God's Passion for You

SAM STORMS

D0994485

KINGSWAY PUBLICATIONS
EASTBOURNE

Copyright © Sam Storms 1998

First published in the USA by Creation House under the title
The Singing God: Discover the Joy of Being Enjoyed by God

First British edition 1998

Unless otherwise indicated, biblical quotations are
from the New International Version © 1973, 1978,
1984 by the International Bible Society. Verses marked
KJV are from the Authorised Version. Crown copyright.
Verses marked NAS are from the New American
Standard Bible © The Lockman Foundation 1960, 1962,
1963, 1968, 1971, 1972, 1973. Verses marked NKJV are from
the New King James Version copyright © 1979, 1980,
1982 Thomas Nelson Inc, Publishers.

ISBN 0 85476 785 1

Designed and produced by Bookprint Creative Services
P.O. Box 827, BN21 3YJ, England, for
KINGSWAY PUBLICATIONS
Lottbridge Drove, Eastbourne, East Sussex, BN23 6NT.
Printed in Great Britain.

Reproduced from the original text by arrangement with
Creation House Strang Communications Company,
600 Rinehart Road, Lake Mary, Florida 32746

Gratefully dedicated to

John Piper,
who thinks God's thoughts,

and

Dennis Jernigan,
who sings God's songs,

and to

Tsianina Storms, my mother,
and *Betty Jane Cawley, my sister,*
who not only filled our home but
our hearts as well with the excellency of worship
and the presence of God.

About the Author

Sam Storms holds a B.A. in History from the University of Oklahoma, a Th.M from Dallas Theological Seminary and a Ph.D from the University of Texas at Dallas.

After pastoring churches in Oklahoma and Texas for nineteen years, he joined the staff as associate pastor at Metro Christian Fellowship in Kansas City, Missouri, in 1993. He also serves as President of Grace Training Centre, Metro Christian's full-time Bible school, of which Mike Bickle is Vice President.

Sam's ministry is characterised by a desire to see the Word and Spirit united in the lives and thinking of all believers. He has a growing desire to see the sick healed and is committed to praying fervently for the release of God's power in this area.

He lives with his wife, Ann, and their two daughters, in Grandview, Missouri.

Contents

Foreword

*I*T IS A SPECIAL PLEASURE for me to recommend Dr. Sam Storms' latest work. I have known Sam for seven years and have worked closely with him at Metro Christian Fellowship and Grace Training Center for the last five of those seven years. During this time I have come to enjoy Sam as one of my favorite preachers in the body of Christ today. His messages regularly challenge my spiritual life and increase my understanding of the beauty of God. Sam has a rare and unique insight into the dynamics of God's kingdom, especially the emotional makeup of God's own personality and His remarkable capacity to enjoy His people.

The reality of a singing God who is filled with abounding passion and delight in His people, yes, even broken people, is the central theme of this book. Sam's skill and knowledge of the Word of God, together with his expertise in church history, have provided him with the tools to speak with persuasion and clarity about this vitally important issue. He esteems the reality and power of our emotions, which reflect the very image of God

Himself, without crossing the line into unbiblical emotionalism. He brings us into the embrace of Jesus, who longs for intimacy with us, without bringing us into a weak sentimentalism in our approach to God.

This book is deeply rooted in the scriptures and in Sam's profound experience of the Lord in his own personal life. Anyone who desires to grow in their passion for Jesus needs to experience the warmth that comes from grasping the beauty and splendor of God's emotional makeup. Although it may sound strange to some, God really does have *feelings for His people*. This book explores in a fresh and revealing way how God experiences inexpressible delight over His children and how you can be touched in the depths of your soul with this life-changing reality.

I can also happily recommend this book because I know the fountain from which Sam drinks. As a close friend and colleague, I have watched his unwavering commitment to biblical orthodoxy and scholarship together with his warm devotion to the person of Jesus and fascination with the unparalleled beauty of the Son of God. Sam is a man who seeks to live and equip the church for a life in the Spirit that is rooted and anchored in the Word of God and the realities of everyday life.

I wholeheartedly recommend this book to anyone who is seeking to make the first commandment first in their life.

—MIKE BICKLE
SENIOR PASTOR, METRO CHRISTIAN FELLOWSHIP
VICE PRESIDENT, GRACE TRAINING CENTER
KANSAS CITY, MISSOURI

A Parable

FOR AS LONG as he could remember the little boy had heard people talking about the Great King. Everywhere he went he listened with rapt attention as they spoke of how big He was and how beautiful and strong. The mere thought of meeting the King set his heart pounding within his chest; his mouth became dry and his palms sweaty. He knew that if he could only see this Great King his questions would all be answered, his fears forever relieved, and his life made full. But he didn't know where to look.

Then one day, quite without warning, the little boy's eyes were opened. He saw light—brilliant, effulgent light. At first he recoiled, afraid. Yet he felt irresistibly drawn forward, ever closer to the light. He had never before seen such a scintillating blaze. The sun was a filthy blotch of black coal compared to this glorious beam.

Something inside said it was the light of the Great King, the light of His eyes and of His countenance. Cautiously, but determined, he followed the light to its source. There upon a throne sat the Great King. It was a throne of such grandeur and glory that the little boy stood stunned and speechless. He glanced around and saw that he was not alone. At the base of the throne had gathered a multitude of others who had also seen the light. They too were in awe of this great and mighty King.

Driven by childlike curiosity he extended his hand and touched the throne. Just as he thought, it was gold. Yet somehow, for all its wealth and worth, it seemed beneath the dignity of Him who sat upon it. Peals of lightning and claps of thunder sounded forth, filling the air with the echo of the King's commands. The little boy had never heard such sounds nor seen such a sight.

From the throne the Great King ruled the worlds. His word stood fast. None dared speak against Him. None dared challenge His decrees. No hand was raised to thwart His will nor word spoken to question His purpose. What a great and powerful King He was! Majesty enthroned!

From the first instant when the boy's eyes fixed on the Great King he wanted nothing more than to obey Him. He was determined to learn all of Him that he could. He studied the King, hoping to measure the dimensions of Him whose length is boundless, whose depth is unfathomable, whose height not even the stars can reach.

The little boy continually read what others had said of the King. He often committed to memory their declarations of His brightness and descriptions of His beauty. Each day the little boy learned something new. His knowledge of the King steadily increased. Others were in awe of the depth of his insight. When they had questions they ran to the little boy for the answer.

The little boy's appetite for information was insatiable. More of the Great King was never enough. With each bit of insight, each item of understanding, his knowledge of the King grew. But the qualities of the King were inexhaustible. After years of looking at the King, listening to the King, reading about the King, and memorizing all that his mind could retain, *the little boy began to grow tired.*

He had seen the King at work and was amazed. He had stood in awe as the King displayed His power in the stars, in the seas, in the souls of men. He had proclaimed to others the majesty and incomparable greatness of the King. But *he was tired.*

On occasion he had even spoken to the King. He told Him how thankful he was for having been brought to the throne and given the privilege of standing in the presence of so grand a Sovereign. But *he was tired.*

He wondered silently, *Is He only a King?* He never questioned the King's right to rule. Nor did he doubt the King's power to enforce His mighty will. Still there was an indefinable hollowness in his heart. Again he wondered, *Is He only a King?*

Then quite unexpectedly, without a word or warning, one day he felt a gentle hand on his shoulder. He felt himself being lifted from the ground, higher, and higher, and higher. The world swirled beneath him as he reached out to grasp something, anything to hold. But he was only to be held.

Then he realized that it was the King who had taken hold of him, drawing him close. The little boy was frightened. He had never been so close to the King. He had been told that the light of the Great King would incinerate and consume him. Yet he felt only quiet warmth, not at all the burning heat of which he had been warned.

There he was, where he never thought he'd be. *Could it really be happening to me? Am I really where I think I am, or is it a dream?* It was no dream, no fantasy. Nothing in his life had ever been so real.

The Great King had stooped and picked up the little boy in His arms, placing him firmly on His lap. And there he sat. The fear was gone. The doubts disappeared.

He felt the arms of tender omnipotence embrace his tiny body, holding him close. He tensed. Would he be crushed? He had seen the King destroy those who turned their backs on the light. Would he soon be among them? No. The embrace was not of judgment but love. The King squeezed the little boy, and he felt himself relax. He knew he was safe. He knew it was okay.

The Great King caressed his forehead and tenderly kissed his cheek. The little boy turned his head, looked up, and gazed into the face of the One he knew as Sovereign. Instead, as his eyes fixed on the Great King's face, he recognized a Father. Was it not the Great King? Yes. And then he knew . . . the Great King was *his* Father, *his* Daddy!

Never before had he known such joy. Not during all the years that he studied about the Great King and talked about Him had he so much as dreamed the King could be so loving. He had always thought of the King in terms of strength and authority. This new experience seemed so out of character. But it wasn't.

He felt the hands of his Father draw him closer still, until his face rested on the breast of this One seated upon the throne. Then he heard it . . . the heartbeat of the Father. The pace quickened. Such throbbing! Such intensity! The little boy feared the Father's chest would burst!

The little boy had heard the rumbling din of volcanic eruptions. He knew the deafening roar of the awesome cataracts of earth. But such sounds were faint and distant whispers when compared with the loving heartbeat of his heavenly Father!

As he gazed into the Father's face he saw what, to his tiny mind, was a paradox—tears poured from the Father's eyes and streamed down across a beaming smile! *How can this be,* he wondered, *that my Father should seem to groan and yet grin at the same time? Why, of course,* said the little boy to himself, *they are tears of joy!*

As he nestled down into his Father's lap, relaxed in the firm embrace that he knew would never let him go, he heard another sound. At first it seemed like humming, soft and slow. Then words . . . the echo of which is now indelibly fixed in his heart. The Father was singing, yes, the Great King. Oh, what a voice! So full, so rich, so pure. The little boy listened ever more intently to hear the words his Father would *sing.*

What? Had he heard correctly? Surely not. But then, there it was again. The same gentle words. The same sweet melody. The same reassuring voice. Over and again, over and again, over and again, his Father was singing, *"My child, I love you!"*

The little boy had been stunned by the brilliance of the light. He had stood in awed amazement of the majestic sweep of the King's sovereign power. But nothing could compare with the joy that rushed gently through his heart when the Father sang once more, "Oh, precious child, how I love you!"

And with that, the little boy fell asleep soundly and safely in his Daddy's arms.

Part One:

The Heartbeat of a Heavenly Father

1

Why This Book Was Written

ONE OF THE MOST bewildering scenes in all the Bible occurred on the eve of Christ's crucifixion. Even though Jesus knew full well that indescribable agony and torture awaited Him, He turned to His disciples and spoke of . . . *joy!* "These things I have spoken to you," said Jesus, "that My *joy* may remain in you, and that your *joy* may be full" (John 15:11, NKJV, emphasis added). Faced with almost unimaginable suffering, Jesus could think of little more than His disciples' *enjoying the joy of being enjoyed by God.*

Jesus knew that once He was gone and the chips were down, when life was hard and the temptation was to give up, only one thing would keep His followers following—*their joy in knowing God's joy in them*. It's no different for us today. The following story is a perfect illustration.

When Susan finally found the courage to get help, she was on the verge of a complete emotional collapse. It wouldn't have been the first time. She had been hospitalized once before and was

15

terrified that if it happened again her family would desert and disown her. "I'm losing control," she said with an unmistakable quiver of fear, "and I don't know what to do."

The scary thing about being a pastor and counselor is that I knew Susan was expecting *me* to know what she didn't. I wasn't altogether grateful for this show of confidence! As I listened to her story I began to feel as helpless as she did.

Susan's father was a demanding tyrant. His so-called "love" for his daughter was cruelly and continually dangled in front of her like the proverbial carrot on a stick. His promises sounded tantalizing to Susan but ultimately rung hollow: *"If* you look pretty, I'll love you. *If* you make good grades, I'll love you. *If* you are successful and helpful and don't embarrass me in front of others, I'll love you."

I'd heard similar stories before. But that didn't make her words any less difficult to endure.

"I was never quite pretty enough, slim enough, smart enough," she said. Susan never did get a bite of that carrot. All she could remember was the bitter aftertaste of her father's disdain and rejection.

Susan and I spent considerable time working through the destructive consequences of her lack of experience with a father's love. But we weren't making much headway. Nothing had the impact we both hoped for until I asked the question: "What does *God feel* when He looks at you?"

"Pity," she snapped back, never pausing to think about it.

"Why?" I asked.

"Because I'm pitiful. I'm pathetic."

For the next hour or so I explained to Susan how much God loves her. I labored at finding just the right words to convince her it was true. It was tough going. I tried images, metaphors, vivid word pictures. They all failed. The idea of a *loving* Father who *enjoyed* her was incomprehensible to Susan. Nothing seemed to make sense.

Then I asked her to read Zephaniah 3:17, "The LORD your God is with you, he is mighty to save. He will take great delight in you, he will quiet you with his love, *he will rejoice over you with singing*" (emphasis added).

"That's how God feels about you, Susan! He looks at you, He thinks of you, and He sings for joy!"

She was stunned. "God *sings*? *God* sings? Over *me*?"

After a few moments of shocked silence tears began to well up in her eyes and stream down her cheeks. "Sam, are you sure?"

"Yeah, I'm sure."

"But I'm so pathetic," she protested. "I really am. I'm thirty pounds overweight, and I'd die if anyone saw the inside of my house right now. It's almost as messy as I am! My husband is furious at me again. I can't do *anything* right. And you say God sings over me with joy? I doubt it! More likely He's screaming in disgust. My dad used to do that."

Again I asked her to read the passage: "The LORD your God is with you, he is mighty to save. He will take great delight in you, he will quiet you with his love, he will rejoice over you with singing."

The tears returned. "If only I could believe it were true. I think then I could face almost anything. If only it were true."

Susan's reaction to Zephaniah 3:17 was dramatic but not unusual. I've seen it again and again. It has led me to a simple but startling conclusion: The only thing that makes life livable is enjoying the joy that comes from knowing one is enjoyed by God.

This in no way minimizes our responsibility to love God. The greatest commandment in the Law is to love the Lord with all our heart and with all our soul and with all our mind (Matt. 22:37). Not loving God is therefore the worst of all human sins. What I have in mind, though, is *His* love for us, *His* deep, emotional, loving movement toward the people He created in His image. So let's not reverse what the Bible sets in order: "This is love: *not* that we loved God, *but that he loved us* and sent his Son as an atoning sacrifice for our sins" (1 John 4:10, emphasis added). Our love for God is a reflex of *His love for us.* He loved us first! We must be careful not to invert the sequence.

I've been a Christian for thirty-eight years. I've been a pastor for twenty-four years. I don't think of myself as old or especially experienced, but I've seen more than I care to remember of human pain and predicaments. I've counseled rebellious teens and lonely senior citizens. I've spent hours with bitter wives and passive husbands. I've cried with victims of sexual abuse and rejoiced with those set free from bondage. Their problems may be different. Some are men; others are women. Some are old, others young. But the one thing they share in common is the most deeply felt need of the human soul: To *know* and *feel* that God loves and enjoys them.

The one thing that gives us hope, that conquers despair, and brings strength for the struggle is the assurance that no matter how bad the problem, God loves us. Pain becomes bearable and tomorrow no longer terrifies when your soul is touched with the reality of God's delight in you. That is why I have written this book.

DOES GOD REALLY CARE?

MANY WILL PROTEST: "But God couldn't possibly love *me*. I'm too small, too insignificant. Why would the Creator of this vast universe of beauty and strength bother to think about *me*? I'm nothing. I've never done anything meaningful. I have no talent. Nobody will notice when I die. Don't patronize me with pious pronouncements about God's love—I've heard it all before."

If you've never had thoughts like this, skip this section. I want to talk briefly to those who were nodding their heads as they read the preceding paragraph. You know who you are. You're the one who goes unnoticed at church. No one bothers to greet you or say hello, except as a formality. You don't believe they mean it. No one shakes your hand, much less hugs you. You're rarely asked to lunch unless you're part of a group that's been invited. No one asks your opinion. No one sits next to you unless it's the only seat left.

It's only natural (though still sinful) to conclude that if people treat me like that, God probably does, too. If that's all I mean to them, it's doubtful I mean much to God either.

When I mentioned to a friend of mine the subject of this book he tried hard, but unsuccessfully, to disguise his disappointment. I asked him about the pained look on his face and encouraged him to be honest with me. He said he had his doubts whether a book on the love of God was really necessary. "Everyone knows God loves them. Why don't you write about prophecy or something that will sell better?"

He was right on one thing: A book on prophecy probably *would* sell better! But he couldn't be more wrong about how people feel God feels about them. Not long after our conversation I was having dinner with another close friend, Dr. Jack Deere. Being the scholar that he is, I was a bit surprised by the simplicity of something he said. "Many in the church today," he said, "are convinced that God is angry with His people. They have no idea *how crazy He is about them!*"

I have to admit it does sound strange to speak of God being *crazy* about His people. But He is! His mind is filled with thoughts of you as He considers fresh and exciting ways to shower you with His good graces. As you drift off to sleep, He is thinking of you. When you awaken, He's still there thinking of you (Ps. 139:18).

If you are still struggling with this, listen to what Jesus said. I think you'll be less inclined to argue with Him about it than you would with me. It is *you* He has in mind when He says:

> Are not two sparrows sold for a penny? Yet not one of them
> will fall to the ground apart from the will of your Father.
> And even the very hairs of your head are all numbered. So
> don't be afraid; you are worth more than many sparrows.
> —MATTHEW 10:29–31

When Joni Eareckson Tada was a little girl, long before the diving accident that left her paralyzed, her parents used to take her to the Baltimore Zoo. For reasons she doesn't entirely understand, her favorite exhibit was the aviary. It wasn't monkeys or lions or bears, but birds that captured her attention. She was captivated by the "brightly-colored parrots, funny-looking toucans, huge, stern eagles, and know-it-all owls."[1] But then, flittering around the outside of the cages, she noticed dozens of common sparrows, finding a home for themselves anywhere they could.

These sparrows weren't important enough to warrant a special cage. No one came to the zoo to see sparrows. They had no extraordinary features or eye-catching colors. As Joni said, "They didn't rate an explanatory plaque. Their pictures didn't appear in the zoo guidebook. Mostly they weren't even noticed."[2]

Sparrows weren't any more valuable in Jesus' day than in Joni's. In fact, sparrows were occasionally used as food for the poor. They were sold two for a penny, approximately one-sixteenth of a man's average daily wage. Hardly in the class of caviar!

Who could possibly care about sparrows today? What value are they to anyone? Yet Jesus says that not one, not even *one*, falls to the ground apart from the will of God. Not so much as one sparrow plummets to the earth unnoticed by its Creator. God cares about His sparrows. He made them. He endowed them with the power to fly. He supplies them with worms and bugs to eat. There are millions upon millions of sparrows in the world, and God knows each by name.

I find it interesting that Jesus chose a sparrow to make His point about how important and valuable you and I are to Him. As Joni said, "He could have used eagles. Or hawks, or falcons, or wide-winged storks. Yet out of the world's nine thousand bird species, the Lord chose one of the most insignificant, least-noticed birds flying around. A scruffy little sparrow."[3]

Why? Because if God is so personally concerned about a creature as unimpressive and insignificant as the sparrow, how much more must He care about the only creatures whom He made in His own image and redeemed by the precious blood of His own Son! If God takes time to oversee the life and demise of a tiny bird, how much more indeed must He watch over *you!*

Jesus puts it even more graphically when He says that "even the very hairs of your head are all numbered. So don't be afraid; you are worth more than many sparrows" (vv. 30–31). There are more than 140,000 hairs on the average head! You may have a few more—I happen to have quite a few less! But God is keenly aware of them all. So if, as you proceed through this book, you find yourself questioning whether God even knows who you are, much less enjoys you, remember the sparrows.

We need to know that God loves us. It's one thing to know

He loves others. I'm good at telling others that. I can accept the fact that God is love and that He delights in pouring out His affection on us. But my heart yearns to feel the gentle and reassuring warmth of His love for *me* with all my faults and failures, with all the secret sins no one else knows about but God, without my first changing and becoming different . . . or better. I need to know that God loves *me* just the way I am now . . . today!

I need to move beyond *hoping* He loves me. Hoping won't do it. Wishing won't do it. Studying about it won't do it. I need to *know,* to be so overwhelmingly assured that nothing can wrench that truth from my soul. My wife, Ann, says she loves me. Her deeds confirm it. She has stayed by my side for over twenty-five years. Yet there's no infallible guarantee that she will be by my side tomorrow. But God will. His love is certain, settled, signed, sealed, and delivered. "Never will I leave you," He says; "never will I forsake you" (Heb. 13:5).

Do you need that kind of a guarantee? Does your heart throb with the desire to be loved like that? Do you yearn to enjoy the joy of God's joy in you? I suspect the answer is *yes* or you probably wouldn't have picked up this book.

If you choose to continue reading you will discover that God not only loves you, now and forever, but that He is *delighted* to do so. He is *ecstatic* in His affection for you. His joy over you is almost too much for Him to bear. He sings and shouts with uninhibited happiness . . . over *you!*

2

God's Passion for His People

WHAT DOES GOD *think* about when He thinks about you? When God meditates on you in His heart, what does He *feel?* When God focuses His eyes on your soul, what does He *see?* When God opens His mouth to speak of you, what does He *say?*

Perhaps many of you would answer those questions like this: "He thinks badly of me; He feels repelled by me. He sees all my ugliness, and He says, 'Yuk!'"

Nothing could be farther from the truth! Notwithstanding what you have been told in the past, or what you may feel in the present, when God thinks about you, feels for you, and sees you, He opens His mouth and sings with inexpressible joy!

God's love for you is so infinitely intense that He quite literally sings for joy. The depth of His affection is such that mere words prove paltry and inadequate. So profoundly intimate is God's devotion to you that He bursts forth in sacred song.

I'm talking about *you*. That's right, *you,* not just all the other people reading this book. I'm talking about each and every one of you who is convinced that no matter how many times I tell you that God loves *you*, still you imagine that God surely has someone else in mind. No, He has *you* in mind.

You may say, "But, Sam, you don't know anything about me. You don't know how ugly I am. You've never been around when I've failed, asked forgiveness, and then failed again ten seconds later. You don't know how poor of a wife (or husband) I've been to my husband (or wife). You've never seen me blow it with my kids, losing my temper and breaking their spirits."

But I don't need to know you. I only need to know God! The issue here isn't who you are or what you've done. It's strictly a matter of who God is—of His character and His determination to love you. Nothing else matters.

Take another look again at Zephaniah 3:17. Observe how it has been translated.

> The LORD thy God in the midst of thee is mighty; he will save, he will rejoice over thee with joy; he will rest in his love, he will joy over thee with singing.
>
> —KJV

> The LORD your God is with you, he is mighty to save. He will take great delight in you, he will quiet you with his love, he will rejoice over you with singing.

> The LORD your God is in your midst, a victorious warrior. He will exult over you with joy, He will be quiet in His love, He will rejoice over you with shouts of joy.
>
> —NAS

After careful study of this verse I've come up with my own paraphrase. It's not a word-for-word translation, but a free and expanded rendering of what I think the original author had in mind. The original Hebrew text isn't as clear-cut as we might hope, and others may differ with my interpretation. But I feel confident that my version will stand up to the scrutiny of study. Here then is my paraphrase of Zephaniah 3:17.

> The Lord your God is with you all the time. He is a powerful and mighty warrior who saves you. When He thinks of you He exults in festive pleasure and with great delight. At other times He becomes quiet as He reflects on His deep affection for you. He celebrates who you are with joyful singing.

Any way you read it the words are stunning. Its force is unmistakable. If ever there were a scripture verse worth committing to memory, this is it. It has rightly been called "the John 3:16 of the Old Testament."

THE FATHER'S PRESENCE

HEAR WHAT IT says about God's *presence*. He is "in the midst of thee," He is "always with you." Just think of it; He is right there where you are, no matter where that may be. That may not get everyone excited, but it sure turned on Zephaniah! His response to God's abiding presence is recorded in verses 14 and 15:

> Sing, O Daughter of Zion; shout aloud, O Israel! Be glad and rejoice with all your heart, O Daughter of Jerusalem! The LORD has taken away your punishment, he has turned back your enemy. The LORD, the King of Israel, is with you; never again will you fear any harm.

There is no way you can tone down this language. You can't escape the uninhibited exuberance contained in these words. Shout for joy! Shout loudly in triumphant exultation! Rejoice and be glad, and celebrate with all your might! *God is with us, so let's party!*

Cast aside all reserve. Forget about what others might think or say. Think about God's presence, His abiding fellowship, and throw caution to the wind! Don't worry about the traditions and formalities of men. Let down your guard for once and be jubilant!

When Zephaniah chose the word *shout* in verse 14 he intended to make a point. This word carries the force of a ringing cry that calls for the onslaught of battle. Observe how it is used elsewhere:

When you go into battle in your own land against an enemy who is oppressing you, *sound a blast* on the trumpets. Then you will be remembered by the LORD your God and rescued from your enemies.

—NUMBERS 10:9, EMPHASIS ADDED

But Joshua had commanded the people, "Do not give a war cry, do not raise your voices, do not say a word until the day I tell you to *shout*. Then *shout!*"

—JOSHUA 6:10, EMPHASIS ADDED

God is with us; he is our leader. His priests with their trumpets will *sound the battle cry* against you. Men of Israel, do not fight against the LORD, the God of your fathers, for you will not succeed . . . and the men of Judah *raised the battle cry*.

—2 CHRONICLES 13:12, 15, EMPHASIS ADDED

In other words, it's okay to get excited about the presence of God. Fill the air with the piercing cry of exultation. Shout for joy! God is with you.

THE FATHER'S POWER

BUT WHAT IF this God can't do anything about my problems? What good is His presence if He isn't strong enough to help me face my struggles?

That's a valid question. Here's the answer: The God who is present with you is also a God of unlimited *power*. He is a mighty warrior, a strong and victorious hero who fights on your behalf.

I know it sounds strange, but think about it anyway. God is a *soldier*! He's dressed for battle, armed, and ready. He is your champion, your defender.

Isaiah exhorts God's people to sing songs of joyful praise, because "the LORD will march out like a mighty man, like a warrior he will stir up his zeal; with a shout he will raise the battle cry and will triumph over his enemies" (Isa. 42:13).

THE FATHER'S PASSION

GOD'S *PRESENCE* COMFORTS ME. His *power* reassures me. But his *passion* overwhelms me. It may make you uncomfortable to hear me say that God is passionate for His people, but there's simply no way to avoid the force of this text. God exults, delights, rejoices, and sings as expressions of His love.

Some theologians insist that God is "impassible," that He does not have passions. I'm sensitive to their concerns. They want to emphasize that God is not weak or mutable or subject to fickle feelings that are provoked by others. I have to agree with them on that point. But it simply won't do to relegate texts such as the following to "figures of speech" or "anthropopathisms."

> "Is not Ephraim my dear son, the child in whom I delight? Though I often speak against him, I still remember him. Therefore my heart yearns for him; I have great compassion for him," declares the LORD.
>
> —JEREMIAH 31:20

> How can I give you up, Ephraim? How can I hand you over, Israel? . . . My heart is changed within me; all my compassion is aroused. I will not carry out my fierce anger, nor will I turn and devastate Ephraim.
>
> —HOSEA 11:8–9

No one fully understands the nature of God's nature. But I do believe God feels. I do believe that God has emotions, passions, affections. In particular, He experiences delight and pleasure, dare I say *ecstasy,* over you and me!

Sherwood Wirt goes so far as to suggest that it was out of *joy* that God created the universe![1] Personally I think he's on to something. When we read Genesis 1:1 and ask *why,* the biblical response is: "So that He might manifest His glory." But why did God wish to manifest His glory? The answer must be because it pleases Him to do so. That is another way of saying *it makes God happy.*

Theologians rarely speak of joy as a divine attribute. They probably think it is beneath God's dignity (or theirs). But Wirt contends that "God's nature expresses itself most characteristically and distinctively through joy."[2] Therefore it was "for His own pleasure and joy" that "in the beginning God created the heavens and earth." God was delighted with the work of His hands and thus pronounced it, "Good!" What He made pleased Him.

If the thought of God's experiencing "pleasure" is a jolt to your religious sensitivities, consider what Jesus said in the parable of the talents: "Come and share your master's [God's] happiness" (Matt. 25:21, 23). God is a happy God.[3] The glory of heaven is wrapped up in our participation in the very joy that floods the heart of the Father. Isn't this why Jesus came? His desire is for the joy of His own life to become the joy of ours (John 15:11).

One can only wonder at the depths of divine delight in the soul of the Son of God. Jesus intends for this very joy to fill up and overflow the hearts of His people (John 17:13). We are to experience not simply joy *in* God or even the joy that God *gives* but better still the very joy that God Himself enjoys. God's joy becomes our joy and in that God takes joy!

All this is just another way of saying that *God is ecstatically happy in His love for His little ones.* If you still balk at such talk, return with me to my paraphrase of Zephaniah 3:17 and look closely at the three statements in the latter half of the verse.

First of all, God "exults over you in festive pleasure and with great delight." What makes this remarkable is that the same language used in verse 14 to describe our rejoicing over God is here used to portray God's rejoicing over us.

We are exhorted to sing. God too rejoices with singing! We are to experience joy. God too delights over us with joy. Back and forth, as it were, God and His people take turns enjoying one another!

All of us know what it's like to get excited about God. We read in Isaiah 61:10, "I delight greatly in the LORD; my soul rejoices in my God" (Isa. 61:10). But God gets just as excited over you, for He Himself says, "I will rejoice over Jerusalem and take delight in my people" (Isa. 65:19).

Better still, God exults over you in "festive pleasure" or with "great delight." How else can I say it? When God thinks about you, His child, His heart explodes in glad celebration. There is divine glee and jubilation beyond words when the almighty God ponders His own.

If you think I'm just making this up, look at how the terms in Zephaniah 3:17 are used elsewhere; ask yourself if "glad celebration" and "glee" and "jubilation" are too strong.

> When the men were returning home after David had killed the Philistine, the women came out from all the towns of Israel to meet King Saul with singing and dancing, with joyful songs and with tambourines and lutes.
> —1 SAMUEL 18:6

> And all the people went up after him, playing flutes and rejoicing greatly, so that the ground shook with the sound.
> —1 KINGS 1:40

Merriment, elation, hoopla, unbridled glee, raucous mirth. That's how we feel about the grace of God and the God of grace. But that's also how He feels about us.

If you are bothered by what seems to be irreverent rowdiness on the part of God, look closely at what comes next in the text. "He becomes quiet as He reflects on His deep affection for you."

Here we see a love that is so deeply felt, so profound, so perfect, that words are inadequate, indeed, unnecessary. To put it bluntly, God is speechless! The all-wise God, the "never-at-a-loss-for-words-God," the God with perfect insight into every situation, the God who always speaks correctly and with divine precision, is here moved to utter silence! Such is the impact of His love for you.

Silence is often the fruit of contentment. When we are unhappy and unsatisfied, we bicker. We bark and we bellyache. But when all is well, when life is what we believe it's supposed to be, we relax in hushed silence. Happiness can express itself not only in loud merriment but also in peaceful quiescence. God is so entirely absorbed in you that He feels no need to say anything!

After the clamorous, yet spiritual, celebration, it is as if God says, "I love you so much that I can't find words to express it. You so perfectly satisfy My every desire and fulfill My every wish that I long simply to embrace you in My arms and quietly enjoy your presence."

One day I was speaking on the telephone with a close friend of mine who was noticeably excited about something she had discovered in God's Word. It seemed to have opened up to her a whole new vista of spiritual insight.

I lost track of the time, but she evidently had been talking, without interruption, for quite a while. I was silent. In fact, she thought I'd hung up! "Sam, are you still there?" she asked.

"Yeah, I'm here," I replied. "I'm just sitting here enjoying you."

I didn't think twice about what I'd just said. Barbara, though, was stunned. She had never given any thought to the idea of "being enjoyed" as a person. That someone might actually take real delight in her was new and even a bit unnerving. She never perceived herself as someone who could evoke that sort of response in another person.

There are times when you think God has "hung up" on you. He's nowhere to be found. Perhaps you suspect He became bored with who you are and what you're doing and moved on to more intriguing people in His kingdom. No! His silence is not a reflection of *disinterest* but *enjoyment*. God is sincerely captivated in His affection for you, and words would only spoil the experience.

God's passionate yearning for you can be both tumultuous and tranquil, celebrative and calm. One moment a party, the next silent and placid.

What imagery! What beauty! I'm stirred by the vision of a husband and wife of fifty years, sitting quietly together at night, rarely speaking, the only sound that of the crackling wood in the fireplace. They are quiet, not because of some emotional barrier between them, but because they know each other so well and are so comfortable in the other's presence that words would disrupt the serenity and tenderness of the moment.

I'm stirred with thoughts of a mother tenderly embracing her young child, rocking gently, softly caressing her forehead, an occasional light kiss on her cheek, without so much as a syllable to disturb the intimacy of her love for that child.

Such is God's love for you!

Palmer Robertson is right. "To consider almighty God sinking in contemplations of love over a once-wretched human being can hardly be absorbed by the human mind."[4]

FROM SILENCE TO SONG

BUT THE SILENCE is eventually broken. Not with cries of disgust. Not with a burst of anger or stinging criticism born of frustration with your failures. But with singing. That's right. God begins to sing, over *you*.

The Search for Extra-Terrestrial Intelligence (SETI) is a ten-year, $100 million program sponsored by NASA whose purpose is to answer once and for all the age-old question: "Is there anyone else out there?"

I first heard about SETI on a TV news broadcast that began with stunning telescopic photographs of distant galaxies. NASA hopes to place in distant space a satellite dish through which to listen for sounds of extraterrestrial life. By the time this book is published such a satellite may well be on its way.

If it were possible to eavesdrop on solar systems millions of light years away, would we hear anything? Is there sound in space?

I believe there is one voice that would indeed be heard. Even now, in the farthest reaches of infinity, among the trillions and trillions of stars yet unseen by human eyes, echoes forth the passionate voice of the Father, singing about His love for you and me.

Loudly and lively, God shouts with joy over His children. He fills the black holes with the light of His love and sings the stars to sleep with lullabies about *you*.

It isn't extraterrestrial life forms that NASA would discover, but the glorious presence of Life Himself, singing in love for His people.

Are you intrigued by the thought of God singing? It makes you wonder: Is He a baritone or a bass?

3

Is God a Baritone or Bass?

*H*E MUST HAVE been about six-feet five-inches tall and weighed in excess of two hundred fifty pounds, every ounce of it muscle. His hair was thick and black. He was wearing a charcoal-gray pinstripe suit and a yellow "power tie." His bearing was dignified and his voice deep, yet mellow and reassuring.

He professed to being a Christian. I had no reason to doubt his salvation, but I had only just met him. My initial concern began as the congregation rose to its feet and began singing "How Great Thou Art." Instead of taking a hymnbook in hand or perhaps singing from memory, he stood erect, arms folded across his massive chest, and kept his mouth shut. It wasn't a defiant stance, but certainly distant and uninvolved.

I never had the opportunity to speak with him about his reasons for not singing in worship with us. But I think I know why. I don't think it was because the musical accompaniment was poor, or because of some inability on his part to carry a tune or read music. I do not believe he was unfamiliar with the songs either.

I discerned that the problem was simply in *singing*. Singing must have been incompatible with his sense of dignity. It required an emotional involvement that threatened the image of strength and self-sufficiency that he was determined to project. Singing demanded a public display of his private devotion. I don't think he was comfortable with his feelings, and the thought of giving vent to them in sacred song was terrifying, even to someone as big and strong as he.

Had he been asked to *speak* about his Christian convictions, I believe he could have spoken without so much as a blink of hesitation. My guess is he could argue, debate, and defend cherished doctrines with the best of them, and that he felt no reluctance at all in doing so. But singing was another matter entirely.

I think singing made him feel vulnerable, bringing to the surface passions that he kept tucked away out of sight. He seemed determined at all costs to stay in control. Singing was no doubt a threat to his resolve to keep a grip on his feelings. It might be okay for women and children, but men are expected to be strong and stoical.

There's simply no denying the vast difference between speaking and singing. It goes beyond the mere fact that some people are embarrassed to sing because they lack a melodious voice.

Music has a peculiar power. Music infuses words with a dynamic energy that merely speaking them could never achieve.

Warren Wiersbe put it this way:

> I am convinced that congregations learn more theology (good and bad) from the songs they sing than from the sermons they hear. Many sermons are doctrinally sound and contain a fair amount of biblical information, but they lack that necessary emotional content that gets ahold of the listener's heart. Music, however, reaches the mind and the heart at the same time. It has power to touch and move the emotions, and for that reason can become a wonderful tool in the hands of the Spirit or a terrible weapon in the hands of the Adversary.[1]

THE SINGING REFORMER

MARTIN LUTHER (1483–1546) is best known for his courageous defense of the doctrine of justification by faith, a truth God used to spark the Protestant Reformation. Yet one of Luther's enemies insisted that he "had damned more souls with his hymns than with all his sermons!" People of every age are compelled to acknowledge the undeniable power of song.

Luther was himself passionately committed to the primacy of music and song as a means both for spreading the gospel and for the worship of God. "I have no use for cranks who despise music," said Luther, "because it is a gift of God. Music drives away the devil and makes people gay; they forget thereby all wrath, unchastity, arrogance, and the like. Next after theology I give to music the highest place and the greatest honor."[2]

Some are surprised to hear what this great theologian thought about music. That a man with such indomitable courage and intellectual brilliance should place such a high premium on song is unexpected, to say the least. "Experience proves," wrote Luther, "that next to the Word of God only music deserves to be extolled as the mistress and governess of the feelings of the human heart. We know that to the devils music is distasteful and insufferable. My heart bubbles up and overflows in response to music, which has so often refreshed me and delivered me from dire plagues."[3]

Luther was never one to mince words. He had little patience for those who dismissed the power and primacy of singing. "He who does not find this [singing] an inexpressible miracle of the Lord is truly a clod and is not worthy to be considered a man."[4] Knowing what I do about Luther, he probably wouldn't have been afraid to say this to the face of our six-foot-five, two-hundred-fifty-pound friend!

Luther insisted that "the gift of language combined with the gift of song was only given to man to let him know that he should praise God with both word and music, namely by proclaiming [the Word of God] through music."[5] Whether you wish "to comfort the sad, to terrify the happy, to encourage the despairing, to humble the proud, to calm the passionate, or to appease those full of hate, name the emotions, inclinations, and affections that impel men to evil or good—what more effective means than music could you find?"[6]

SINGING VERSUS SPEAKING

WHAT LUTHER HAD discovered was that singing enables the soul to express deeply felt emotions that mere speaking cannot. Singing channels our spiritual energy in a way that nothing else can. Singing evokes an intensity of mind and spirit. It opens the door to ideas, feelings, and affections that otherwise might have remained forever imprisoned in the depths of one's heart.

Singing gives focus and clarity to what words alone often make fuzzy. It lifts our hearts to new heights of contemplation. It stirs our hope to unprecedented levels of expectancy and delight. *Singing sensitizes.* It softens the soul to hear God's voice and quickens the will to obey.

I can only speak for myself, but when I'm happy I sing. When my joy increases it cries for an outlet. So I sing. When I'm touched with a renewed sense of forgiveness, I sing. When God's grace shines yet again on my darkened path, I sing. When I'm lonely and long for the intimacy of God's presence, I sing. When I need respite from the chaos of a world run amok, I sing.

Nothing else can do for me what music does. It bathes otherwise arid ideas in refreshing waters. It empowers my wandering mind to concentrate with energetic intensity. It stirs my heart to tell the Lord just how much I love Him, again and again and again, without the slightest tinge of repetitive boredom.

THE SINGING GOD

ALL WELL AND GOOD, you say. But what's the point? The point is this: *God sings, too!*

Sure He speaks. He tells us what to do. His voice fills the air. He declares and denounces and proclaims and whispers. But best of all, *He sings!*

Why should we find that hard to swallow? Adam heard God

speak in Eden. Moses quaked at God's voice on Sinai. Jesus and John the Baptist listened as the words echoed across the waters of the Jordan River: "This is my Son, whom I love; with him I am well pleased" (Matt. 3:17).

If God can speak, why can't He sing? We know He loves music. More than eighty-five times in the Old Testament alone either we are commanded to "sing" praises to God or we read about someone else doing it to His delight.

What must God's voice sound like? Several years ago Ann and I were privileged to hear well-known opera singer Luciano Pavarotti sing in Tulsa, Oklahoma. There's something about a live concert that cannot be captured on CDs and television broadcasts, no matter how great the media quality. Beverly Sills sings with incomparable beauty. Some prefer the passion of Dennis Jernigan or the wide range of country star Leann Rimes.

I wonder what God's voice sounds like when He breaks forth in song. Bass? Tenor? Baritone? Or is there some indefinable blending of each? Or must we presume that the singing God sounds anything remotely like singing man? What do you hear when you envision God's singing? John Piper answered that question for himself:

> I hear the booming of Niagara Falls mingled with the trickle of a mossy mountain stream. I hear the blast of Mount St. Helens mingled with a kitten's purr. I hear the power of an East Coast hurricane and the barely audible puff of a night snow in the woods. And I hear the unimaginable roar of the sun, 865,000 miles thick, 1,300,000 times bigger than the earth, and nothing but fire, 1,000,000 degrees of centigrade on the cooler surface of the corona. But I hear this unimaginable roar mingled with the tender, warm crackling of logs in the living room on a cozy winter's night.[7]

Aside from the *sound* of the singing God, *what* does He sing and *why*? That's easy. He sings of His love for you. Why? Because He loves you!

Here is the crowning jewel of Zephaniah 3:17: God loves you

with such emotional vitality that "He celebrates who you are with joyful singing!"

"Joyful singing" is the translation of one Hebrew word that appears several times in the Old Testament. It literally means a "ringing cry," but should not be thought of as an inarticulate shriek or scream. When the choir of Jehoshaphat belted out a "ringing cry" it was the substantive declaration, "Give thanks to the LORD, for his love endures forever" (2 Chron. 20:21). God's people are exhorted to "tell of his works with songs of joy" (Ps. 107:22; cf. also Ps. 105:43; 126:2; Isa. 12:6; 35:10). This requires articulate utterance.

Earlier we saw that God's love for His children often reduces Him to silence, to quiet, contemplative affection. I remember when our two daughters were quite young that Ann would rock them to sleep each night. Although she will be the first to admit her voice is not operatic, both Melanie and Joanna would insist she sing to them. The gentle hush of a mother's passion would then be broken by the sound of song—love songs for her offspring.

God too shatters the silence with His own songs of delight. What possibly could stir the mighty God of heaven and earth to sing? Not *what* but *who*—you! God's delight is over *you*. *You* make Him glad. He is overjoyed with *you*. *You*, His child, are the apple of His eye, the choicest among ten thousand.

My love for my two girls is virtually inexpressible. I enjoy them. I relish their presence. I adore them. I cherish every word they speak. I treasure their souls. I appreciate their efforts, even when they fail. I dote on them in public. I am devoted to their immediate and ultimate welfare. I am passionately in love with them both.

But God loves me more! God loves you more! Our love for our own children pales in comparison with the passion of the Father for His little ones.

A LOVE BEYOND BELIEF?

I KNOW IT sounds too good to be true. In fact, knowing what we do of ourselves, it sounds ridiculous. When I tried to explain

God's love to a young lady named Karen, she could only s̲. her head in disbelief.

Karen is married and the mother of three children. As she tells it, her principal struggle in life has always been eating. She is at least one hundred pounds overweight and has nothing but contempt for herself. Karen has tried dozens of weight-loss programs, only one of which proved successful for a time.

She lost over fifty pounds and appeared to be on her way to a much healthier life. But she recalls looking at herself in a mirror and saying, "I'm still fat and ugly. I may weigh less, but I'm still the contemptible failure I've always been." Knowing she felt that way about herself, it didn't surprise me when the weight returned.

All her life Karen had been told, "You *are* what you do. You *are* what other people perceive you to be. You *are* how you appear." Performance, and especially physical beauty, became the measure of personal value. "How can God love me," she asked one day, "when I've got my head buried in the refrigerator? How can God love me when I'm eating everything but the plastic wrappers?"

It seemed as if Karen had every excuse in the world to question the truth of Zephaniah 3:17. "Repeated failures and repulsive fat would hardly provoke anyone to sing," she insisted. It was just more than she could handle. "Love like that exists only in fairy tales," she once told me.

A STARTLING DISCOVERY

PSALM 103 HAS always been one of my favorites. I've read it dozens of times, but it wasn't until recently that I saw something that took my breath away. Look with me at verses 10–13.

> He has not dealt with us according to our sins, nor rewarded us according to our iniquities. For as high as the heavens are above the earth, so great is His lovingkindness toward those who fear Him. As far as the east is from the west, so far has He removed our transgressions from us. Just

as a father has compassion on his children, so the LORD has
compassion on those who fear Him.

—NAS

How high are the heavens above the earth? A million miles? A
billion? A trillion? Try infinity! If you could quantify God's tender-
heartedness for you and me, that's about as close as one could come
to making sense of it. Even then the infinity of space is a paltry
comparison to the incomprehensible extent of God's love.

Let's try again. You go east and I'll go west, not on earth, but
into space. Don't stop. Now, when do you think we'll see each
other again? Silly question, isn't it? The answer, obviously, is
never! That's precisely when you will see the guilt of your sin
again: *never!* Catch your breath, and let's do it one more time.

I'm speaking to moms and dads now. How much do you love
your kids? To what lengths would you go to protect and provide
for them? How deep is your compassion when they hurt?
Multiply that by forever. Such is God's compassion for those
who fear Him.

What one thing makes it hard to believe that any of this is
true? I can only answer for myself, but for me it's what I know
about my own heart. Every moment of every day I'm confronted
by the ugliness of my soul, my tendency to wander from God, my
calloused preoccupation with no one but myself, and it sickens
me. So what must God think? After all, He's omniscient. He
knows me far better than I know myself. He sees the sins that I
conveniently deny. He knows the "thoughts and intentions of the
heart" (Heb. 4:12, NAS), and that scares me. Thinking about
God's thinking about me threatens to overturn everything the
psalmist has said. But then comes verse 14 of Psalm 103. Even
now when I read it, I struggle with disbelief: "For He Himself
knows our frame; He is mindful that we are but dust" (NAS).

It seems only reasonable that God's knowledge of my "frame"
would end all hope of intimacy with Him. How could God
possibly draw near to me, knowing me as He does? It is because we
think this way that we run *from* God rather than *to* Him when we
sin. Yet look closely at what the psalmist says: It is *because* God is

mindful that you are but dust that He loves, forgives, and shows compassion. I know that sounds horribly illogical. Common sense tells us that God's knowledge of who we are must drive Him away. But Psalm 103 says precisely the opposite!

Don't miss the little word "for" that opens verse 14. What a stunning little word. It's only one word, but it will turn your entire grasp on who God is and how He relates to you upside down. My earthly mind tells me that it is precisely *because* God knows my frame that He would want nothing to do with me. Intimate and uncomfortably specific insight into the sinful propensity of our souls is the very thing we think would make it impossible for God to feel anything but revulsion when He looks at us. But the psalmist says it is *because* God has such knowledge that He chooses not to reward us according to our iniquities, but rather to shower us with loving-kindess, compassion, and forgiveness.

You are dust. I am dust. We are all frail, forgetful, ungrateful, weak, finite creatures, formed from the dust of the earth. Worse still, when we mix in the reality of sin, our dust turns to mud. God knows it all, *and for that reason* shows loving-kindness beyond measure and mercy forever. It may not seem sophisticated to do so, but all I can say is, "Wow!"

One word of caution, though. None of this means that God approves of our sin, only that His love is *greater* than our sin. Our weakness and wretchedness are no barrier to His sovereign grace. Paul says the same thing in Romans 5:6–8. He anticipated that some of his opponents would use this magnificent truth to justify their wickedness. Does this concept about God's love as found in Psalm 103, Romans 5, and elsewhere mean that we are "to continue in sin that grace might increase?" (Rom. 6:1, NAS). God forbid! "May it never be!" declares Paul. "How shall we who died to sin still live in it?" (Rom. 6:2, NAS).

The point is this: *Your knowledge that God's knowledge of you moves Him to compassion ought to move you to commitment.* Anything less is unacceptable.

Some may still find it too much to swallow. Karen did. "There are just too many strikes against it," she said, on the verge of despair. There was a time when I struggled with this too, until

John Piper pointed out to me that God has Himself taken steps to overcome every obstacle.

I ask, "Can you feel the wonder of this today—that God is rejoicing over you with loud singing?"

"No," you say, "I can't, because I am too guilty. I am unworthy. My sin is too great, and the judgments against me are too many. God could never rejoice over me."

But I say, "Consider Zephaniah 3:15. God foresees your hesitancy. He understands. So His prophet says, 'The LORD has taken away His judgments against you' (NAS). Can you not feel the wonder that the Lord exults over you with loud singing today, even though you have sinned? Can you not feel that the condemnation has been lifted because He bruised His own Son in your place, if you will only believe?"

"No," you say, "I can't, because I am surrounded by enemies. Obstacles press me in on every side. There are people who never let me believe this. There are people at work who would make my life miserable if God were my treasure. There are people in my family who would ostracize me. I have friends who would do everything to drag me down. I could never go on believing. I would have too many enemies. The oppression would be too much to bear. I could never do it."

But I say, "Consider Zephaniah 3:17, 'The LORD . . . is a . . . warrior' (NAS) who gives victory; and verse 19, 'At that time I will deal with all who oppressed you,' says the Lord; and verse 15, 'He has cast out your enemy' (NKJV). Can you feel the wonder that God is doing everything that needs to be done for you to enjoy His own enjoyment of you? Can you see that the enemies and the oppressors are not too strong for God? Nothing can stop Him when He exults over you with loud singing. Can you feel the wonder of it now? Can you believe that he rejoices over *you?*"

"No," you say, "still I can't, because He is a great and holy God, and I feel like He is far away from me. I am very small. I am a nobody. . . . "

But I say, "Consider Zephaniah 3:15, 'The King of Israel, the LORD, is in your midst' (NAS); and verse 17, 'The LORD your God is in your midst' (NAS). He is not far from you. Yes, I admit that this staggers the imagination and stretches credibility almost to the breaking point—that God can be present personally to everyone who comes to Him and believes on Him. But say to yourself, again and again, 'He is God! He is God! What shall stop God from being close to me if He wants to be close to me? He is God! He is God! The very greatness that makes Him seem too far to be near is the greatness that enables Him to do whatever He pleases, including being near to me. . . . '"

But still you say, "No, you just don't understand. I am the victim and the slave of shame. I have been endlessly belittled by my parents . . . I have been scoffed at and threatened and manipulated and slandered. Inside this cocoon of shame even the singing of God sounds faint and far away and indecipherable. It is as though my shame has made me deaf to anyone's happiness with me, especially God's. I cannot feel it."

But I say, "I am sure I do not feel all that you feel. I have not been through what you have been through. But God is no stranger to shame. Unbelievable shame was heaped on His Son (Heb. 12:2), terrible slander, repeated belittling, even from his own townsfolk (Matt. 13:55–58). Therefore, 'We do not have a high priest who is unable to sympathize with our weaknesses' (Heb. 4:15). I know I have never walked in your shoes. I did not have to live with the family you lived with.

"But Jesus knows. He feels it with you. And best of all His Father says, right here in Zephaniah 3:19, '*I will save the lame and gather the outcast, and I will turn their shame into praise and renown in all the earth*' (NAS). Is it not amazing how well God knows you? Can you not feel the warmth of His heart as He makes provision for every question you have? Do you not yet hear the singing of God as you draw near?"[8]

That's what this book is all about: Hearing in your heart the heavenly aria of God's unfathomable love for *you*. He doesn't just say it. He doesn't just write it. He doesn't just tell others who in turn pass the word on to you. God *sings* to you, "I love you, oh, how I love you! My child, I love you!"

Part Two:

Love Songs of the Almighty

4

The Obscenity of the Cross

*D*ON'T LAUGH, but I proposed to my wife on our first date. Oh well, go ahead and laugh. After twenty-five years of marriage it even strikes me as silly.

It wasn't actually a proposal; it was more a comment to the effect that I was convinced God had introduced me to the girl I was supposed to marry. Ann still gets a kick from telling people about it. If you're finished laughing we'll move on to the serious point of the story.

The fact is, selecting a mate for life is no laughing matter, especially if the person you've selected says *no!* I'm eternally grateful Ann said *yes!* She's everything I ever wanted in a wife—and more.

My point is simply this: I asked Ann to marry me (on our first date and then again one year later) because I was convinced that she would be the best wife any man could hope for. It never entered my mind to propose marriage to other women I'd met and known. Ann was kind, pure, gentle, loving, and wholeheartedly committed—first to God, and to me second.

Twenty-five years of marriage haven't changed her.

That's why I read the Old Testament story of Hosea with shock and amazement. Hosea may have lived twenty-seven hundred years ago, but his idea of marriage wouldn't have differed greatly from mine. Like most other men, he wanted a wife who was faithful, pure, gentle, and loving. He didn't get one.

Hosea married a prostitute. Hosea's wife, Gomer, was a whore, a harlot. She was unfaithful, ungrateful, unbelieving, and unloving. Why, then, did he marry her? Because God told him to do so.[1]

> Go, take to yourself an adulterous wife and children of unfaithfulness, because the land is guilty of the vilest adultery in departing from the LORD.
>
> —HOSEA 1:2

Hosea was to represent God. Gomer, his wife, was to play the part of Israel. Instead of simply telling His people how sinful they were and how He was determined to love them anyway, God brought Hosea and Gomer center stage to act it out dramatically.

So Hosea married a harlot. He adopted the children she had conceived because of her immoral trysts (Hos. 1:2). She then bore Hosea three children whom God also used to illustrate the depth of Israel's sin.

I'm fascinated with the reasons people give for naming their children as they do. Often names are selected that the parents hope will instill confidence in their children. Other parents pick whatever names are fashionable at the time. I happen to be named after my grandfather.

My father once told me of a family in his hometown who named their six children Victor, Vada, Vida, Velda, Vester, and Vernon! A friend of mine, less concerned with alliteration, opted for biblical names for his seven kids.

When God named the offspring of Hosea and Gomer, His decision was shaped by the lessons He wanted to teach Israel. Thus the firstborn, a son, was named *Jezreel*, which means "God scatters." This clearly pointed to the judgment that would befall

Israel. The second child was a daughter, *Lo-Ruhamah*, which means "not pitied." The third child, another son, was called *Lo-Ammi*, "not my people."

Marriage and motherhood did nothing to temper Gomer's promiscuous passions. She cheated on Hosea. She turned her back on him, spurned his love, and committed adultery.

Love, like most everything else, surely has its limits. Who would dare speak ill of Hosea if he had divorced Gomer for her infidelities? But he didn't. God's love, symbolically expressed in the action of Hosea, *unlike* everything else, shatters the mold. Indeed, it stretches the limits of credulity.

How can I even begin to describe a love so deep that it would pursue a chronic fornicator even as she seeks illicit pleasures in the arms of her paramour? Yet that is precisely what God told Hosea to do!

> The LORD said to me, "Go, show your love to your wife again, though she is loved by another and is an adulteress. Love her as the LORD loves the Israelites, though they turn to other gods and love the sacred raisin-cakes." So I bought her for fifteen shekels of silver and about a homer and a lethek of barley. Then I told her, "You are to live with me many days; you must not be a prostitute or be intimate with any man, and I will live with you."
>
> —HOSEA 3:1–3

Hosea, playing the part of God, was to purchase back to himself his wayward and wanton wife. Gomer, playing the part of unfaithful Israel, is redeemed by the relentless love of her husband.

Moreover, the threats implied in the names of their children are graciously transformed into blessings. The power of God's love is such that *Jezreel* no longer means "God scatters" but "God plants" (Hos. 2:22). *Lo-Ruhamah* becomes *Ruhamah*, "pitied." And *Lo-Ammi* becomes *Ammi*, "My people."

Make no mistake. The redemptive love of Hosea for Gomer, that is, of God for Israel, was a foreshadowing of God's love for the church, for *you* and *me*. Let me be blunt: *You and I are spiritual fornicators*. We are worthy of eternal divorce in the depths of hell. But "this is how God showed his love among us: He sent his one and only Son into the world that we might live through him. This is love: not that we loved God [any more than Gomer loved Hosea], but that he loved us and sent his Son as an atoning sacrifice for our sins" (1 John 4:9–10).

Gomer was redeemed by Hosea for fifteen shekels of silver and a homer and a lethek of barley. God redeemed us through the precious, spotless blood of His dear Son, Jesus Christ (1 Pet. 1:18–19)! Indeed, "God demonstrates his own love for us in this: While we were still sinners, Christ died for us" (Rom. 5:8; cf. John 3:16; Gal. 2:20; Eph. 5:2).

Merely sending Jesus into the world could hardly be construed as an act of unparalleled love. But sending Him to die as the redemptive price for the souls of scurrilous spiritual adulterers like you and me is love beyond degree.

FOR GOD SO LOVED THE WORLD

JOHN 3:16, SURELY the most famous verse in the Bible, makes this point precisely. Unfortunately though, many have missed the meaning of this remarkable text altogether.

We are told often that God's love is great because it extends to each and every person who has ever lived. "Just think," so it is said, "of the multitudes of men and women who have swarmed across the face of the earth. Oh, how great the love of God must be to embrace within His arms this countless multitude of people."

But I'm not so sure. I'm not convinced that we learn much about God's love by counting heads. God's love is magnified not when we ask *how many?* but when we ask *what kind?* That is, the issue is not *quantity* but *quality*. The *nature* of the people God loves is crucial, not their *number*.

The highlight of John 3:16 is that God has loved the *world*. The contrast is *moral*, not *mathematical*. The difference between God and the world isn't that He is one and it is many. The point John makes is that He is *holy* and the world is *sinful!* That's what makes His love for the world so astounding.

God's love for the world is remarkable because the Lover is righteous and the beloved is not. He who dwells in unapproachable light has entered the domain of darkness. The just has died for the unjust (1 Pet. 3:18). In other words, we marvel at John 3:16 because it tells us that God has loved the *moral antithesis* of Himself.

When the apostle John uses the term "world," both here and throughout his writings, he portrays it as sinful, estranged, alienated from God, and subject to His curse. The world is detestable because it is the contradiction of all that is holy, good, righteous, and true. The world is that system of fallen humanity viewed *not* in terms of its *size* but as a satanically dominated rebellion at war with the kingdom of Christ.

The point, then, is *not* that the world is *so big* that it takes a whole lot of love to love it all. The point is that the world is *so bad* that it takes an amazing love to love it at all.

The Obscenity of the Cross

THE LOVE OF the Lord Jesus Christ for His bride, the church, is nowhere more vividly seen than in the horrors of the cross He willingly endured on her behalf. Many, however, know virtually nothing of the cross and its significance as the token of God's love. We sing about the cross. We wear it dangling from our neck or wrist. We emblazon it across the top of our church letterhead, but I wonder how much we really understand what it means to say that Jesus was impaled on one.

There is no escaping the fact that nearly two thousand years of pious Christian tradition and religious art have largely domesticated the cross. The cross of Jesus has been sanitized and stripped of its original meaning. No matter what you and I think we know about crucifixion as a means of capital punishment, the cross simply does not mean the same for us today that it did for those who witnessed the scene as Jesus was being nailed to one.

I remember when the state of Oklahoma executed its first death-row inmate after the Supreme Court lifted its ban on capital punishment. Debate was intense and focused primarily on the most "humane" way to inflict death. Every effort was made to minimize the man's pain and to diminish any humiliating or embarrassing factors. The electric chair was thus replaced with death by lethal injection.

It hasn't always been this way. In the ancient world crucifixion was employed precisely *because* it was unparalleled in its capacity to inflict pain and lingering agony, precisely *because* it was humiliating and embarrassing.

It comes as quite a surprise to many people when they discover that the four Gospels say virtually nothing about the crucifixion of Jesus. In all four accounts of His death, we read simply that "they crucified him" (Matt. 27:35; Mark 15:24; Luke 23:33; John 19:18).

The reason is that people in the first century were all too painfully familiar with the details of crucifixion. It wasn't necessary for the gospel writers to be any more precise than they were.

Each day when I leave the church to go home I pass a number of stores, restaurants, and gas stations. Nothing exceptional. Nothing offensive. Just so, people in Jesus' day would close their shops, head for home, and often pass by a row of crucified victims left for days on their respective crosses. They knew all they wanted to know about such horrors.

What exactly did they see? They saw crosses in various shapes: some in the form of an *X*, an uppercase *T*, and often the more familiar lowercase *t*. The victim's feet would be no more than one to two feet above the ground, making it possible for scavenger dogs to feed on the corpse. One ancient author wrote:

> Punished with limbs outstretched, they see the stake as their fate; they are fastened and nailed to it in the most bitter torment, evil food for birds of prey and grim pickings for dogs.[2]

In 1968 in a Palestinian cemetery, a bulldozer accidentally unearthed the skeletal remains of a man who had been crucified. According to one description, "The feet were joined almost parallel, both transfixed by the same nail at the heels, with the legs adjacent; the knees were doubled, the right one overlapping the left; the trunk was contorted; the upper limbs were stretched out, each stabbed by a nail in the forearm."[3]

The man's right tibia, the larger of the two bones in the lower leg, had been brutally fractured into large, sharp slivers. Although this victim had been hung by nails through the forearms, it is possible to hang someone by nails through the palm, contrary to what some have said. If the nail enters the palm through the thenar furrow it breaks no bones and is capable of supporting several hundred pounds.

Often a small peg or block of wood, called a *sedecula*, was fixed about midway up the vertical beam, providing a seat of sorts. Its purpose was to prevent premature collapse. In other words, it was designed to prolong the agony of the victim.

Debate still rages on the precise cause of Jesus' death. Some argue that He died from asphyxiation. Others insist it was loss of blood, whereas shock seems most likely.

It is hard to imagine a more hideous form of capital punishment. If ever there were a true deterrent to crime, it was crucifixion. Historians find it strangely ironic that Julius Caesar was hailed as being merciful to his enemies in that he ordered their throats to be cut prior to crucifixion to spare them the indescribable suffering of prolonged agony on the tree.

Here's where most Christians stop, if they get this far at all. I realize such descriptions are not pleasant reading. But if all you know of the cross is the physical pain it inflicted, you have yet to understand the depths of Christ's love. Let me explain.

In 1 Corinthians Paul describes the message of the cross as "foolishness" to unbelieving Gentiles and a "stumbling block" to Christ-rejecting Jews (1:18, 23). Does Paul mean that the cross is *intellectually incoherent*, like saying two plus two equals five? Is he suggesting that the cross is *religiously illogical*, like saying that salvation is both by grace and works? No. The message of forgiveness through the cross of Christ is foolishness because of what the cross meant to the ancient world. It was the embodiment and emblematic symbol of the worst of human obscenities.

Someone was once asked to define *obscene*. He replied, "I can't define it, but I know it when I see it!" I agree. When confronted with something obscene we experience an intuitive revulsionary reaction. Our sense of personal dignity is offended; decency is besmirched; and we feel emotional anguish. Something need not be sexual to be obscene. Anything that is abhorrent, repulsive, or disgusting qualifies. An obscenity, whether seen or spoken, violates our sense of aesthetic and social propriety.

I think Paul is saying that the cross of Jesus Christ was obscene! It was far more than an instrument of capital punishment. It was a symbol of personal reproach, public indecency, and social indignity. If all they wanted to do was kill Jesus, they could have stoned him (like Stephen) or decapitated him (like James).

Crucifixion, on the other hand, was specially designed to do more than kill a man. Its purpose was to humiliate him as well. Crucifixion not only broke a man's body, it crushed his spirit. Crucifixion not only destroyed a person physically, it defamed him socially. As difficult as this may be for you and me to understand, worse than the suffering of the cross was its *shame*.

Specific steps were taken to ensure its shame. Crucifixion was always public. We argue today over whether or not executions should be televised. In the ancient world there was no debate. The most visibly prominent place was selected—at a crossroads, in the theatre, on a hill (like Calvary). Why? To intensify the victim's personal humiliation.

People were always crucified naked, although Jewish sensitivities demanded they be provided a loin cloth. John Calvin describes the significance of this:

> The Evangelists portray the Son of God as stripped of His clothes that we may know the wealth gained for us by this nakedness, for it shall dress us in God's sight. God willed His Son to be stripped that we should appear freely, with the angels, in the garments of His righteousness and fulness of all good things, whereas formerly, foul disgrace, in torn clothes, kept us away from the approach to the heavens.[4]

The first Adam, originally created in the righteousness of God, did by his sin strip us naked. The last Adam, suffering the shame of nakedness, did by His obedience clothe us in the righteousness of God!

What the ancient world thought of crucifixion is seen in the way it received treatment in their literature. Historians used to think that the scarcity of references to the cross in cultured literary sources was evidence that it was rarely employed as a means of execution. But now we know that the cross was infrequently mentioned because most refined authors refused to disgrace and soil their work by so much as mentioning something as vile and obscene as crucifixion!

No wonder Pliny the Younger (A.D. 112) called Christianity a "perverse and extravagant superstition" because it preached Christ crucified.[5] Christians were accused of being overcome by a "sick delusion" for daring to suggest that God had been nailed to a cross! This may well be the reason Saul of Tarsus (later the apostle Paul) vigorously opposed the church, "breathing out murderous threats" against the believers (Acts 9:1; cf. Acts 8:3; 22:4; 26:11; Gal. 1:13).

Opposition to the gospel wasn't due primarily to the claim that Jesus was God in the flesh or because the church was a threat to ancient religious customs or because the life of Jesus failed to conform with messianic expectations. The principal stumbling block was that Jesus had been *crucified!*

A "crucified Messiah" was a contradiction in terms. One may have a Messiah, or one may have a crucifixion, but one cannot have a crucified Messiah. The Messiah is the embodiment of power, splendor, and triumph. Crucifixion is the embodiment of weakness, degradation, and defeat.

To be crucified was to fall under the curse of Deuteronomy 21:23: "Anyone who is hung on a tree is under God's curse" (cf. Gal. 3:13). A person executed by some other means or who may have fallen in battle would be hung on a tree as a sign of God's ultimate curse.

Thus what Saul heard (and himself later preached) was that He who was to enjoy God's richest blessing instead endured God's most reprehensible curse! How could these Jews honor as God one whom God himself had openly and obviously condemned?

Worse than a contradiction in terms, a "crucified Messiah" was an outrageous blasphemy to religiously minded Jews.

The offense of the cross, therefore, arose from the fact that the cross itself was a visible symbol and physical embodiment of that which was morally shameful and aesthetically repugnant. To suggest that the "Lord of glory" was nailed to the cross of shame was the height of folly.

This explains why Paul was himself so horribly and viciously denounced and persecuted for preaching "Jesus Christ and him crucified" (1 Cor. 2:2; cf. Gal. 6:14). Paul makes the point clearer still in the famous Christ-hymn of Philippians 2:6–11. He refers to Jesus:

> Who, being in very nature God, did not consider equality with God something to be grasped, but made himself nothing, taking the very nature of a servant, being made in human likeness. And being found in appearance as a man, he humbled himself and became obedient to death—even death on a cross!
>
> —PHILIPPIANS 2:6–8

Don't miss the connection Paul draws between the Son's taking on the form of a slave, or servant, and His dying on a cross. Crucifixion was reserved for slaves, for the riffraff of society, the dregs and refuse of the world. We must never forget that the death Jesus died was the vilest indignity to which the most reprehensible social pariah could be sentenced.

Thus, "*even* death on a cross" (Phil. 2:8, emphasis added) is the last bitter consequence of taking the very nature of a slave/servant and stands in the most abrupt and shocking contrast imaginable with "being in the very nature God" (v. 6).

Jesus Christ suffered not only for our sins but for the *shame* of our sins as well. Such was the depth of our depravity and the magnitude of his love.

So the next time you are depressed and feel abandoned, and are desperate for some assurance that God really loves you, fix your eyes on "the old, rugged cross—the emblem of suffering and shame." That is how much God loves you.

Can you hear Him singing?

5

Orphans to Heirs

$\mathcal{E}$VERY ONCE IN A WHILE we need to be reminded how incredibly good God is. We also need to be reminded how much God enjoys being good. We need to be told of the unfathomable depths of delight in God's heart when it comes to His treatment of His children. God really is good, and He really does delight in doing good to those who are His own.

You may think that sounds a bit trite, even trivial. After all, it's one of the first things we learn when we become Christians, one of the fundamental lessons we learn in Sunday school. But at the same time it's also one of the most difficult truths for Christians to believe.

Many Christians live in fear that God really isn't good at heart and has little desire to do good things for them. I'm not trying to be cynical. I only wish to acknowledge openly what I know for a fact is churning inside your own soul.

Ask yourself a simple question: "Have you found what you've read to this point a little beyond belief? Is the idea that God loves you so much that He sings a bit preposterous?" Go ahead and say *yes*. No one can hear you but God, and He understands your doubts.

Perhaps our skepticism comes from seeing so much evil in the world. We look around, perhaps even at our own lives, and think, *If God is really good, why is the world filled with so much rot? Why is my life such a hopeless mess?* Or maybe we think, *If God is good, He's only good to good people. And since I'm no good, God won't be good to me.*

That's why we need daily reminders of how incredibly good God is. Jesus certainly knew that to be true. That's why He said to His disciples (then and now):

> Do not be afraid, little flock, for your Father has been pleased to give you the kingdom.
>
> —LUKE 12:32

John Piper explains:

> Every little word in this stunning sentence is intended to help take away the fear that Jesus knows we struggle with, namely, that God begrudges His benefits; that He is constrained and out of character when He does nice things; that at bottom He is angry and loves to vent His anger. This is a sentence about the nature of God. It's about the kind of heart God has. It's a verse about what makes God glad—not merely about what God *will* do or what He *has* to do, but what He *delights* to do, what He *loves* to do and takes *pleasure* in doing.[1]

Look closely at one part of this verse. Jesus says that the Father "has been pleased" to give us the kingdom. "Has been pleased" uses the Greek verb *eudokeo*.

This particular verb is found only six times in the four Gospels. What makes its usage in Luke 12:32 significant is the fact that in each of the other five places where it occurs the word is being spoken by the Father as He speaks about Jesus, His Son.

At the baptism of Jesus, "a voice from heaven said, 'This is my Son, whom I love; with him I am *well pleased*'" (Matt. 3:17, emphasis added; cf. Matt. 12:18; Mark 1:11; Luke 3:22). On the Mount of Transfiguration Peter was silenced by the Father and told to listen to the Son, with whom the Father is "*well pleased*" (Matt. 17:5).

Jesus selected the verb *eudokeo* for a reason. It is the word He heard His Father use to express His feelings to Him, the Son. So Jesus says to them, "Do you remember Me telling you about My baptism, the dove, and the voice from heaven? Do you recall what I told you My Father said about His love for Me? *That's how He feels about you, too!*"

Let's stop and catch our breath! The more I meditate on this the more unbelievable it becomes! Yet, there Jesus says it in words that no one can escape: "God is as happy and delighted about giving you the kingdom, with all its blessings, as He is about My doing what I'm doing in fulfillment of His will!"

That's how much God enjoys doing good things for you and me. That's how much He loves us!

The Father is well-pleased with Jesus because He was everything a Father could want in a Son. He was perfectly obedient to the Father's will (John 5:19–21; 8:28–29) and always sought the Father's glory (John 17:4). Besides, the Father simply enjoyed the fellowship that He and the Son shared. In other words, the Father loved the Son (John 5:20)!

I'll be the first to admit that the relationship between the Father and Jesus the Son is unique in many ways. After all, this is a matter of God's loving God. Jesus is the special, only begotten Son of God (John 1:14, 18).

Still, though, Jesus knew this when He selected this one word *eudokeo* to describe how the Father feels about doing good to you and me. I can't escape concluding that what this means is that as God delights in Jesus, as He is pleased and happy with and thrilled by His Son, so He is happy and excited and pleased about giving you and me all the blessings of His blessed kingdom!

All of us know about the joys of giving. Have you ever received a gift from someone only to respond by saying, "It's so beautiful, so exquisite, but I can't accept this. It's just too much."

Invariably the giver's countenance falls. He is brokenhearted. Why? Because you have robbed him of the joy of giving. His joy in giving comes from your joy in receiving. If you don't joyously receive, it spoils *his* delight in *your* delight.

The fact is, sometimes we don't trust givers. When someone gives us a present or treasure, and then another, then another, and still one more, our initial joy turns to suspicion. We say to ourselves, *She must have some ulterior motive. She's getting ready to spring the trap on me. She's setting me up for something with all these gifts.*

Perhaps so. But not God! He gives and gives and gives because He enjoys giving. *He enjoys the joy you get from getting what He gives!* The only thing God has up His sleeve is another gift! Such is the nature of divine love.

THE GIFT OF SONSHIP

SO WHAT IS God's greatest gift? What is the most exquisite blessing in the kingdom that God is "well pleased" to bestow?

Is it justification? Is it forgiveness? Perhaps eternal life? What about the Holy Spirit whom God has given to dwell in our hearts?

I don't like comparing God's gifts, and I certainly don't want to suggest that these blessings are anything but precious and perfect. But I want us to consider what may well be God's second greatest gift (next to that of His Son's dying for our sins). Except for the demonstration of God's love on the cross of Calvary, in my opinion the most marvelous proof of God's love for you and me is this: *Adoption. Sonship.* The right and privilege and authority that has been given to us to become the children of God.

Observe the apostle John's words:

> How great is the love the Father has lavished on us, that we should be called children of God! And that is what we are! . . . Dear friends, now we are children of God, and what we will be has not yet been made known. But we know that when he appears, we shall be like him, for we shall see him as he is.
>
> —1 JOHN 3:1–2

The tone of John's words virtually bristle with urgency and excitement. "Come quickly and see! Look! Listen! You can't imagine what I have to tell you!"

I like that. Here's an elderly man nearing the end of life who still gets excited about the love of God.

Why? Because John knew that God's love has bestowed on us the greatest of all blessings: *sonship*. Here is the measure of God's love. Here is the test of how deeply He treasures us.

The biblical doctrine of adoption makes sense only when we remember that we are not God's natural children. It is true that God is the Father of all men and women insofar as He is the Creator. But many such "children" of God will spend an eternity in hell. One does not become a spiritual child of God by being *born*, but by being *born again*. Let me explain.

My heart breaks each time I see or read about the orphans in such lands as Romania and Afghanistan. Communist oppression has taken its toll on countless little children who have been cruelly abandoned. They are alone, discarded, often diseased and deformed, helpless, and without hope.

It isn't a pretty picture. It's just as ugly when looked at spiritually. For we are all born *spiritual orphans*. Apart from Jesus Christ we too are abandoned and stricken with a fatal disease called *sin*. We have no family, no father, no future.

Here is where God's incalculable love makes its appearance. Listen again to the words of the apostle:

> He [Jesus] was in the world, and though the world was made through him, the world did not recognize him. He came to that which was his own, but his own did not receive him. Yet to all who received him, to those who believed in his name, he gave the right to become children of God—children born not of natural descent, nor of human decision or a husband's will, but born of God.
>
> —JOHN 1:10–13

John is describing the glorious truth of our adoption as sons and daughters into the family of God. Paul speaks often of this as well:

For you did not receive a spirit that makes you a slave again
to fear, but you received the Spirit of sonship. And by him
we cry, "Abba, Father." The Spirit himself testifies with our
spirit that we are God's children.

—ROMANS 8:15–16

You are all sons of God through faith in Christ Jesus.

—GALATIANS 3:26

This latter declaration of Paul's makes it inescapably clear:
There is no saving relationship to God as Father without a living
faith in Jesus Christ.

Being a child of God, therefore, is not a universal status
everyone attains by natural birth. It is rather a supernatural gift
one receives by believing in Jesus. Adoption is wholly and utterly
an act of God's spontaneous and uncoerced love.

J. I. Packer reminds us that in the ancient world "adoption was
a practice ordinarily confined to the childless well-to-do. Its
subjects . . . were not normally infants, as today, but young adults
who had shown themselves fit and able to carry on a family
name in a worthy way. In this case, however, God adopts us out
of free love, not because our character and record show us worthy
to bear His name, but despite the fact that they show the very
opposite. We are not fit for a place in God's family; the idea of
His loving and exalting us sinners as He loves and has exalted
the Lord Jesus sounds ludicrous and wild—yet that, and nothing
less than that, is what our adoption means."[2]

Even today when a childless couple visits an orphanage with a
view to adopting, they invariably base their choice on physical
beauty and intellectual skills. Rarely does one hear of a child
with Downs syndrome being adopted. Rarely does the orphan
with spina bifida go home with new parents.

Prospective parents want to know about a child's natural father
and mother. Was this child the product of rape? What is his ethnic
origin? Did she come from "good stock?" What is his IQ?

God's choice of us is utterly and eternally different. He didn't
make us His children because we were prettier than others.

Divine adoption isn't concerned with physical health or financial wealth or potential or one's past history. God loves the unlovely and unappealing. God loves because God loves. That is why you are His child. Because He loves you.

John goes to great lengths to insist that entrance into God's family is on a different plane from entrance into one's earthly family. (See John 1:10–13.) One does not become a child of God by the same process one becomes a child of a physical parent. In other words, spiritual life is not genetically transmitted!

My earthly father was a Christian. So too is my mother. But that isn't why *I* am a Christian. Your father and mother may not be Christians. But that has no ultimate impact on whether or not you are.

The DNA of one's parents has nothing to do with becoming a child of God. Your heritage, ancestry, family tree—no matter how glorious and impressive—have nothing to do with your entrance into heaven. The fact that you have descended from noble blood or are the product of peasants is irrelevant. I'm proud of the name "Storms." But when I stand before God He says, "Who?"

Being adopted into God's family is one of the most glorious blessings a good and loving God could possibly bestow. I rejoice in the fact that I've been justified and forgiven and granted eternal life. But to know and experience God as my Father, Abba, Daddy, is greater still.

When you are justified by faith in Christ, you stand before God as Judge and hear Him declare, "Not guilty! Righteous through faith in Jesus!" Praise God! But in adoption, God the Judge steps down from behind His legal bench, removes His stately robes, stoops down, and takes you into His arms of love, saying softly, "My son, my daughter, my child!"

I relish the experience of every divine blessing. I thank God daily that I am a member of the body of Christ and a citizen of the kingdom. But nothing can quite compare with knowing that when I was homeless, helpless, and hopeless, God rescued me from the gutter of sin and made me His child. Nothing can compete with the thrill of being adopted as a full and coequal heir with Christ Jesus (Rom. 8:17).

I've seen this kind of love illustrated by Roger and Paula, who, having been told by several physicians that they would never conceive a child, adopted four kids. Sure enough, Paula later conceived and gave birth to a beautiful baby girl. But she is no more or less loved than the other four. Together they all bear the family name and stand to inherit the family estate.

So too in God's family. Says Packer, "God receives us as sons, and loves us with the same steadfast affection with which He eternally loves His beloved only begotten. There are no distinctions of affection in the divine family. We are all loved just as fully as Jesus is loved. . . . This, and nothing less than this, is what adoption means. No wonder that John cries, 'Behold, what manner of love!' When once you understand adoption, your heart will cry the same."[3]

It isn't make-believe. It is more real than you can ever imagine. To every soul that doubts, to every heart that wonders if it's only a name, a label, with no substance, John reassuringly declares, "And that is what we are!" (1 John 3:1). It's fact. It's truth. It's reality.

Oh, yes, there's one more thing. Neither John nor Paul nor any other biblical author says that we are God's "foster" children. We are His *adopted* children. The former relationship is at best a temporary one. The latter is eternal.

TWICE ADOPTED: A LOVE STORY

OVER THE YEARS I've observed that Christians who've come to grips with having been adopted by their earthly parents frequently display unusually perceptive insight into spiritual adoption. It certainly makes sense to me. To be the recipient of such marvelously unsolicited love from people who are not one's biological parents must be a tremendous thrill.

I've sensed this time and again from one young lady who was adopted at birth. Her appreciation for having been adopted into God's family is understandably immense. She seems to rejoice in this glorious spiritual truth on a level yet unattained by most of us. I have learned much from her as she has shared with me her thoughts on the subject. I think you will, too.

JANIE'S STORY

JANIE'S BIOLOGICAL MOTHER already had four children, and for reasons of her own felt compelled to give up her fifth for adoption. From the moment Janie entered her new home she began to learn about the kind of love God has for His adopted children.

The love her new parents had for her could hardly have been greater had she been their biological child. Nowhere is this better seen than in the saying Janie's new mom kept on her noteboard. It read:

> Not flesh of my flesh,
> Nor bone of my bone,
> But still miraculously my own.
> Never forget for a single minute,
> You didn't grow under my heart—
> But in it.

It's a bit difficult for me to explain how Janie must feel, so I asked her to put it in her own words. Her words confirmed the fact that adopted children often have a special appreciation for the truth of spiritual adoption.

"Being adopted," explains Janie, "gives me an unusual ability to understand my adoption into God's arms. My parents had no idea whether I would be a boy or girl. They wanted me regardless of my gender. God also loves us irrespective of gender. Knowing that they loved me before I was born deepens my gratitude that God knew me and chose me before the foundation of the world!

"My adoptive parents chose to ignore my impoverished past. The fact that my natural mother was on welfare didn't diminish their love for me. Likewise, God knows our wicked past, our spiritual impoverishment, down to the smallest disgusting detail.

Yet He loves us anyway! To have been twice adopted and loved in this way goes beyond any words in my vocabulary."

Janie brought me a copy of the final adoptive decree and pointed out a fascinating and instructive paragraph. It states, "For all intents and purposes whatsoever, the said child is and is hereby declared to be in the same relationship to the Petitioners [the adoptive parents] as if born to them by natural birth, and remaining in such relationship as if the child were their own. . . . "

What this means, among other things, is that Janie is legally as much a child of these parents as any other born to them by natural means. She is a coheir with all others in that family. We too are coheirs with Christ, our brother. The good news is, whereas this earthly adoptive decree is stamped and notarized by the state, our "spiritual adoptive decree" is sealed with the blood of Christ and signed by the God who cannot lie!

Whereas sometimes the love of earthly parents falters and even fails, the love of our heavenly Father is immutable. No one in heaven or on earth can challenge the eternal legality of what God has done for us by making you and me His beloved children.

Janie also pointed out yet another statement in the decree that says, "The rights of all other persons, if any they have, to the care, control, and custody of said child be and the same are hereby forever and finally terminated." If you can't get beyond the legal language, listen to how Janie explains it.

> These words can be used to describe God's adoption of me into His family. When I was adopted by my earthly parents, my old identity was terminated. Legally speaking I became a new and different person. I became Mary Jane Fox. When I was adopted by my heavenly Father I also left behind my old self and was reborn with a new identity, a clean slate, a fresh start.

Recently I rejoiced with Janie and her husband as they celebrated the birth of their first child. At one point Janie said, "She is so fragile and vulnerable! She stumbles and falls and whines and often makes such a mess of things. But that's the way we are with God. Every day I stumble and fall and mess things up, but my Father is there to pick me up. He comforts me when I'm down. I complain and get into trouble. Yet He gently corrects me and loves me in a way that overshadows even the best of earthly affections."

Earthly adoptive love is unspeakably special. Yet such sacrifice and passion, for all its beauty, for all its wonder, pales before the brilliant light of God's love for you and me, one-time spiritual orphans. "How great is the love the Father has lavished on us, that we should be called children of God! And that is what we are!" (1 John 3:1–2).

Like I said, every once in a while we need to be reminded how good and loving God is. So how good and loving is He? "How great is the love the Father has lavished on us [*you*]," cries John, "that we [*you*] should be called children [*a child*] of God!"

Can you hear your Father singing over His children? Can you hear Him singing over *you?*

6

A Clean Slate

*H*E SHOULD HAVE known better. He never should have stayed at home alone while his army was fighting in the field. He never should have lingered late at night on his rooftop. He never should have set his eyes on that beautiful lady. He never should have inquired about who she was, nor should he have sent for her, nor should he have slept with her. He should have known better.

But King David sinned, and Bathsheba conceived.

He should have known better. He never should have tried to force Bathsheba's husband, Uriah, to sleep with her, hoping that he would think the child was his own. He never should have arranged for Uriah's death. He should have known better.

But King David sinned, and Uriah died.

He should have known better. Having committed adultery with Bathsheba he should have acknowledged his sin to the Lord. But he didn't. Having conspired to kill Uriah, her husband, he should have confessed his transgression. But he didn't.

He kept quiet about his sin. He suppressed it. He shoved it

deep down inside, thinking it gone for good. He ignored the tug on his heart. He denied the pain in his conscience. He numbed his soul to the persistent pangs of conviction.

Then one day the prophet Nathan told David a story. It was all about a rich man who stole the one little ewe lamb of a poor man rather than taking a sheep from his own huge flock. "Surely this man deserves to die!" shouted an enraged David.

With a bony finger pointed at David's nose, Nathan calmly declared, "You are the man! . . . Why did you despise the word of the LORD by doing what is evil in his eyes? You struck down Uriah the Hittite with the sword and took his wife to be your own" (2 Sam. 12:7, 9).

David should have known better.

Adultery and murder make for a sensational story. Many a television miniseries has rocketed to the top of the Nielsen ratings on the wings of those two sins. Rarely, though, does Hollywood portray the anguish and turmoil they inflict. Listen to what David says in Psalm 32 about the impact of his sin as it festered unconfessed and unforgiven in his heart. Then listen more closely still to the song of God's forgiving love.

SIN SUPPRESSED

> When I kept silent, my bones wasted away through my groaning all day long. For day and night your hand was heavy upon me; my strength was sapped as in the heat of summer.
>
> —PSALM 32:3–4

Someone described David's anguish as "the inner misery of the lacerated heart." David "kept silent" about his sin. He ignored the voice of the Holy Spirit and suppressed the piercing conviction that stabbed repeatedly at his conscience. He refused to deal openly and honestly and forthrightly with God. He would not face his sin. He was living under the delusion that if *he* could somehow forget about it, God would, too.

David portrays the impact of his sin in physical terms. Some think this is metaphorical language, that David is using physical symptoms to describe his spiritual anguish. Whereas that's possible, I suspect that David was feeling the brunt of his sin in his body as well.

What we see here is a law of life in God's world. If you bottle up sin in your soul it will eventually leak out like acid and eat away at your bones. Unconfessed sin is like a festering sore. You can ignore it for a while, but not forever.

The physical effects of his spiritual choices are agonizingly explicit. There was *dissipation:* "My bones wasted away" (cf. Ps. 6:2). There was *distress:* "my groaning all day long." And David was *drained:* "My strength was sapped as in the heat of summer." Like a plant withering under the torrid desert sun, so too was David dried up and drained out from suppressing his sin.

In other words, he was quite literally sick because of his refusal to "come clean" with God. His body ached because his soul was in rebellion. Spiritual decisions always have physical consequences. "The Spanish Inquisition," wrote Charles Spurgeon, "with all its tortures was nothing to the inquest which conscience holds within the heart."[1]

God simply will not let His children sin with impunity. It was, in fact, *God's* hand that lay heavily on David's heart. To sin without feeling the sting of God's disciplinary hand is the sign of illegitimacy. (See chapter eight.)

All of us can identify with David's reluctance. No one likes to admit being wrong. No one enjoys confessing error, far less something as serious as adultery and murder.

Our younger daughter, Joanna, was seven years old when she faced the task of putting together her first science fair project. It wasn't an especially difficult assignment. She was to plant some beans in a jar, supply them with sufficient water and sunlight, and then answer the simple question, "Will they sprout?"

After asking everyone in the family their opinion, she opted to say *no.* The next morning she hurriedly rushed to the jar to discover, to her utter dismay, that the beans had indeed sprouted. She was told that the final part of the project was to record her findings.

"Write down, 'I was wrong about the beans,'" her mother said.

"No! I won't say I was wrong!"

"But Joanna, you *were* wrong. You said the beans wouldn't sprout, but they did. So write it down."

"No! I won't say I was wrong!"

"Joanna!"

"No!"

We were at an impasse. Her determination amazed us. Something inside that little soul recoiled with a ferocious refusal to openly acknowledge error. The project was in jeopardy. We were at our wit's end when her older sister, Melanie, came to the rescue. A veteran of numerous science projects, she had figured out a way to resolve the problem.

"Joanna, you don't have to say you were wrong. Just write, 'My hypothesis was erroneous.'"

Undoubtedly without so much as a clue to the meaning of those words, Joanna shouted, "Yeah! That sounds okay."

No one, neither a seven-year-old first-grader nor the king of ancient Israel, relishes the thought of confession. Facing our faults, whether intellectual as in Joanna's case, or moral as in David's, is terribly discomforting.

But here is the good news! Psalm 32 is not primarily about the agony of denial and the pain of repression. It is about the joy and blessedness of forgiving love!

SIN CONFESSED

Blessed is he whose transgressions are forgiven, whose sins are covered. Blessed is the man whose sin the LORD does not count against him and in whose spirit is no deceit. . . . Then I acknowledged my sin to you and did not cover up my iniquity. I said, "I will confess my transgressions to the LORD"—and you forgave the guilt of my sin.

—PSALM 32:1–2, 5

You talk about confession! David ransacks his dictionary for every word for sin he can find. He calls what he did a *transgression*

(v. 1), a word that refers to the rebellious and disloyal nature of his actions. He calls what he did a *sin* (v. 1), a word that points to any act that misses the mark of God's revealed will. And he calls it *iniquity* (v. 5), that is to say, a crooked deed; a conscious intent to deviate from what is right.

Why do you think David goes to such verbal lengths to portray his sin? My sense is that he does so to emphasize that *every* sin, *any* sin, whatever its cause or character, no matter how small or big, secret or public, intentional or inadvertent, *all* sin can be forgiven!

David also uses three different words to describe his confession. He *acknowledged* his sin to the Lord. He refused to *cover up* his iniquity. He was determined to *confess* his transgressions (v. 5).

Nothing is held back. There is no cutting of corners. No compromise. He comes totally clean. All the cupboards of his soul are emptied. All little black books are opened and read aloud. His confession is like opening the floodgates of a dam. It may be messy at first, but the release of ever-increasing pressure is life to his burdened heart.

Three different words for sin. Three different words for confession. But better still, three different words for forgiveness!

Blessed is the man whose transgressions are *forgiven* (v. 1). The word literally means "to carry away."

David's sin, my sin, *your* sin, is like an oppressive weight from which we long to be relieved. Forgiveness lifts the burden from our shoulders.

Blessed is he whose sin is *covered* (v. 1). It is as if David says, "Oh, dear Father, what joy to know that if I will but uncover my sin and not hide it, You will!"

David doesn't mean to suggest that his sin is merely concealed from view but somehow still present to condemn and defeat him. The point is that God sees it no more. He has covered it from all view.

Blessed is that man or woman, young or old, whose sin the Lord does not *impute* or *count* against them (v. 2). No record is kept. God isn't a spiritual scorekeeper to those who seek His pardoning favor!

The Joy of Forgiveness

HAVE YOU EVER fooled around with an "Etch-a-Sketch?" I never was much good at it. I'm not an artist by any stretch of the imagination. The Etch-a-Sketch was made for people like me. If you don't like what you've drawn, and especially don't want to be embarrassed should anyone else see it, you simply tip the screen and your work of art vanishes!

It's a crude and simple illustration, but that is a lot like what God does with your sin when He grants forgiveness. Through the course of our earthly existence we sketch an ugly scenario of sin and rebellion and ingratitude and jealousy and lust. There it is, vividly imprinted on the screen of our souls.

But when we confess our sin, as David did, God's loving and gracious hand tips the toy, and the slate is wiped clean! No matter how often we return to deface our lives with ugly pictures of hatred and anger and pride and envy, God is faithful to tip the screen. All it takes is confession. All it takes is the blood of Christ.

But don't take my word for it. Listen to what God Himself says: "I, even I, am he who blots out your transgressions, for my own sake, and remembers your sins no more" (Isa. 43:25). When we confess our sin and plead the blood of the Lord Jesus, God promises never again to bring it up, either to Himself, to you, or to others. That's forgiveness! That's love!

God's not finished yet. He's got another illustration to make His point. Hezekiah put it this way:

> Surely it was for my benefit that I suffered such anguish. In your love you kept me from the pit of destruction; you have put all my sins behind your back.
>
> —ISAIAH 38:17

God has taken your sin and placed it out of sight behind His back. All He sees now when He sees you is the blessed righteousness of His own dear Son, the Lord Jesus Christ. Such is the love of forgiveness.

Still not good enough? Still not convinced? Still afraid that your sins will do you in? Then pay close attention to the word of the prophet Micah. He has something important to say about the kind of God we have.

> Who is a God like you, who pardons sin and forgives the transgression of the remnant of his inheritance? You do not stay angry forever but delight to show mercy. You will again have compassion on us; you will tread our sins underfoot and hurl all our iniquities into the depths of the sea.
>
> —MICAH 7:18–19

How much more graphic do you demand God be before you enter into the joy of His forgiving love? All vestige of condemning guilt is gone. Again, "Just as God said He *put* our sins behind His back, so here He says He will *hurl* them into the depths of the sea. They will not 'fall overboard;' God will hurl them into the depths. He wants them to be lost forever, because He has fully dealt with them in His Son, Jesus Christ."[2]

Like you, I watched with amazement as the latest underwater technology scoured for remains of the Titanic, recovering from the bottom of the sea what everyone thought lost forever. No! No! It won't happen with your sins! The submarine has not been made that can submerge that deep. The equipment has not been found, and never will be, that can retrieve the slightest vestige of your transgressions. God forbids it. Such is the quality of His forgiving love.

I don't know how all this affects you, but I agree with David when he says (shouts?), "Blessed is he whose transgressions are forgiven . . . Blessed is the man whose sin the LORD does not count against him . . . " (Ps. 32:1–2).

All hope for happiness is contingent on the forgiveness of sins. The word *blessed,* by the way, is plural! As Spurgeon has said, "Oh, the blessednesses! the double joys, the bundles of happiness, the mountains of delight" that abound to the forgiven.[3]

Having experienced for himself the joy of forgiving love, David encourages others to seek God's pardoning favor:

Therefore let everyone who is godly pray to you while you may be found; surely when the mighty waters rise, they will not reach him. You are my hiding place; you will protect me from trouble and surround me with songs of deliverance.

—PSALM 32:6–7

God is like a high rock on which we stand when the flood waters of adversity begin to rise.

God is a hiding place, a shelter in whom we find safety and protection from all that threatens the soul.

And remember, He is all this for men and women like David who have spurned His ways and transgressed His will!

What accounts for this willingness in God to forgive? To what do we attribute the peace and release and joy that floods the pardoned soul?

David puts his finger on it in verse 10: "Many are the woes of the wicked, but the LORD's *unfailing love* surrounds the man who trusts in him" (emphasis added). God's love is the bulwark of our lives, the bodyguard of our souls, the atmosphere of immutable affection in which we move and live and breathe.

THE POWER OF FORGIVING LOVE

THE LIFE-CHANGING power of God's forgiveness is oblivious to national and ethnic boundaries. Consider the experience of Ah Ping, a young boy who grew up on the streets of Hong Kong.[4]

At the age of twelve, Ah Ping was initiated into the Triads, a wide-ranging criminal society that exerted its power through Chinese youth gangs. The Triads ruled the streets of Hong Kong, especially in the infamous Walled City of Kowloon. They controlled the drug traffic, loan sharking, prostitution, pornography, vice dens, protection rackets, and every imaginable illegal activity.

When he was only fourteen, Ah Ping was supported financially by a teenage prostitute who sold herself in exchange for his physical protection. His reputation as a street fighter had grown, and he was feared by many.

In 1965 Jackie Pullinger, a young British missionary, walked into the Walled City with the gospel of Jesus Christ. She opened a youth club in the very heart of what was at the time the most corrupt and debauched city on earth.

Ah Ping was a frequent visitor. One night he sensed Jackie's frustration and said, "You'd better go. You'd better leave this place. You should find a nice group of well-behaved students to preach to. We're no good. We never do what you want us to do. I don't know why you stay here. You find us schools, but we don't attend. You find us homes, but we destroy them. You find us jobs, but we lose them. We won't ever change. All we do is take what you give and kick you around. So why do you stay? What's the point?"

"I stay because that's what Jesus did for me," said Jackie. "I didn't want Jesus, but He didn't wait until I wanted Him. He didn't wait until I had promised to reform. He didn't wait until I got good. He died for me anyway. He died for me when I hated Him, and He never even 'told me off' on the cross; He just said He loved me and forgave me. Jesus is the Son of God. And He loves you, too."

Ah Ping was incredulous. "No way! It can't be. Nobody would love us like that. I mean, we . . . " His voice faltered. He regained control of himself. "I mean, we rape and fight and steal and stab. Nobody could love us."

It wasn't easy, but Jackie did her best to explain to Ah Ping that Jesus didn't love what he did, but who he was. She explained the death of Jesus for sinners and the forgiveness that comes through simple faith.

Ah Ping was shattered. "He could hardly believe there was a God like that," Jackie later wrote. "He sat down there on the stone steps to the street and told Jesus that although he could not understand why He loved him, he was grateful; and he asked Jesus to forgive him and change him."[5]

This fourteen-year-old gangster was the first fully initiated Triad to become a Christian through Jackie Pullinger's ministry. The shocking reality of God's forgiving love had penetrated the hardened crust of his criminal heart and made him a new creature in Christ.

The joy of forgiveness impelled Ah Ping to bring his Triad brothers to the youth club. He insisted that Jackie tell them about the love of Christ. At the time he had no idea that his own commitment to the God who had forgiven him would soon be severely tested.

One evening Ah Ping was attacked by a gang of youths who beat him mercilessly with wooden bats. They left him unconscious with a deep gash in his back and a hole in his throat. Ah Ping's former gang brothers vowed to avenge the assault. "No," said Ah Ping, "I'm a Christian now, and I don't want you to fight back." A new creature indeed!

WHO LOVES MORE?

FORGIVENESS IS A powerful force. It never leaves the forgiven unchanged. Dan Allender is on target in saying that "the extent to which someone truly loves will be positively correlated to the degree the person is stunned and silenced by the wonder that his huge debt has been canceled."[6]

A case in point is the story of the ex-prostitute who crashed a dinner party being held in Jesus' honor. The presence of uninvited guests wasn't unusual. They would normally line up around the table, their backs against the walls of the home, listening to the dinner conversation and even asking a question or two of the guest.

But what Luke describes in chapter seven of his Gospel record is utterly out of the ordinary. This is the home of Simon, a Pharisee, a respectable and reputable religious leader. It never crossed anyone's mind that a woman of such "low class" would have the gall to enter. But it wasn't gall that compelled her. It was love.

We are told that when she learned of Jesus' presence in Simon's house "she brought an alabaster jar of perfume, and as she stood behind him at his feet weeping, she began to wet his feet with her tears. Then she wiped them with her hair, kissed them and poured perfume on them" (Luke 7:37–38).

Her original plan was to anoint Jesus' head with the perfume, but her emotions got the better of her. If Jesus was reclining on a cushion, as was the custom, her tears would naturally fall on His feet. In her anxiety to make up for the mishap, she ignored every rule of ancient etiquette and let down her hair and wiped His feet dry. Then, in deep reverence and gratitude, she anointed His feet and kissed them repeatedly. *Everything* she did was exceptional and out of the ordinary and indicated that something remarkable had occurred in her life.

Simon is appalled! Jesus comes quickly to her defense. He tells a parable of two men who owed some money to a moneylender. One owned a large sum, the other a small sum. Because neither had the money to repay their debt, the moneylender forgave their debts. Then Jesus turned to Simon and asked, "Who will love more, Simon, the person who has been forgiven little or the one forgiven much?" (See verse 42.) Simon is stuck. So he says, "I suppose the one who had the bigger debt canceled" (v. 43). At least Simon got one thing right that night!

Then Jesus makes His point. "Therefore, I tell you, her many sins have been forgiven—for she loved much. But he who has been forgiven little loves little" (v. 47). Forgiveness is not the *reward* for love, but its *fruit*. Jesus is not stating the cause of forgiveness but the fact that it has already occurred. Love is the living witness to a heart set free!

Perhaps you haven't sinned as David did, nor as Ah Ping or the woman of Luke 7. Adultery, murder and prostitution may not be on your list. Perhaps your sins are more subtle and less public, whether fewer or greater in number. Whatever the case, David's only hope, Ah Ping's only hope, the weeping ex-prostitute's only hope—your only hope—is the unfailing love of God.

7

How Long Will Love Wait?

I DON'T USUALLY CRY when I read, but I wept over *Come Back, Barbara.*[1] They were tears of grief, of fear, and of joy. That may sound like a strange combination, until you hear the story that John Miller and his daughter Barbara tell of eight tumultuous and ultimately triumphant years in their relationship.

Miller, a Presbyterian minister, and his wife, Rose Marie, have five children. When their daughter Barbara turned eighteen, she angrily turned her back on virtually everything her parents held dear. She repudiated Christianity and mocked the values it embodied. For the next eight years her life was a roller-coaster ride of drugs, alcohol, immorality, marriage, divorce, and remarriage.

I cried with grief as John Miller opened his broken heart to let others in. I cried with fear as I thought of my own two daughters and the potential in them to walk the same path Barbara Miller chose for herself. I cried with joy as John and Barbara described her reconciliation with God and family.

I have good reason for mentioning (and recommending) this

book. It is a brutally honest, true-grit, modern-day example of the truths expressed in the parable of the prodigal son (Luke 15:11–32). In his foreword to the book Larry Crabb writes that "too many prodigal-son (or -daughter) stories have little of the realism of the biblical version, the horror of sin, and the painful eagerness of a parent longing for the child's return."[2] But this one does.

As I read this story I couldn't help but think of the anguish in God's heart when we stubbornly demand what we think we deserve and then squander God's gifts in sinful excess. But then I thought of something even more incredible: the patience of divine love that waits with open arms for the return of the prodigal child.

THE PARABLE OF THE PRODIGAL SON'S FATHER

LET'S LOOK AGAIN at what may be the most famous story Jesus ever told. You may be surprised by what you see.

> There was a man who had two sons. The younger one said to his father, "Father, give me my share of the estate." So he divided his property between them.
>
> Not long after that, the younger son got together all he had, set off for a distant country and there squandered his wealth in wild living. After he had spent everything, there was a severe famine in that whole country, and he began to be in need. So he went and hired himself out to a citizen of that country, who sent him to his fields to feed pigs. He longed to fill his stomach with the pods that the pigs were eating, but no one gave him anything.
>
> When he came to his senses, he said, "How many of my father's hired men have food to spare, and here I am starving to death! I will set out and go back to my father and say to him: Father, I have sinned against heaven and against you. I am no longer worthy to be called your son; make me like one of your hired men." So he got up and went to his father.
>
> But while he was still a long way off, his father saw him and was filled with compassion for him; he ran to his son,

threw his arms around him and kissed him.

The son said to him, "Father, I have sinned against heaven and against you. I am no longer worthy to be called your son."

But the father said to his servants, "Quick! Bring the best robe and put it on him. Put a ring on his finger and sandals on his feet. Bring the fattened calf and kill it. Let's have a feast and celebrate. For this son of mine was dead and is alive again; he was lost and is found." So they began to celebrate.

Meanwhile, the older son was in the field. When he came near the house, he heard music and dancing. So he called one of the servants and asked him what was going on. "Your brother has come," he replied, "and your father has killed the fattened calf because he has him back safe and sound."

The older brother became angry and refused to go in. So his father went out and pleaded with him. But he answered his father, "Look! All these years I've been slaving for you and never disobeyed your orders. Yet you never gave me even a young goat so I could celebrate with my friends. But when this son of yours who has squandered your property with prostitutes comes home, you kill the fattened calf for him!"

"My son," the father said, "you are always with me, and everything I have is yours. But we had to celebrate and be glad, because this brother of yours was dead and is alive again; he was lost and is found."

—LUKE 15:11–32

Of all our Lord's parables, many would claim this as their favorite. Yet amazingly it is one of the most misunderstood passages in all of Scripture!

Contrary to what you've read and contrary to the numerous sermons you've heard on this text, the main point of the story is not the *sin* of the son but the *love* of his *father*. Most have argued that the point of the parable is the behavior of the younger of the two brothers. The message, they insist, concerns the need for repentance regardless of how deep into sin one may have fallen.

A few contend that the parable is primarily about the older brother and the rebuke he received for not rejoicing over his sibling's salvation. He is said to be representative of the scribes and Pharisees who refused to acknowledge Jesus' seeking and saving sinners.

We can certainly learn a lot from the behavior of both brothers. But I'm convinced the focus of the story is on the prodigal son's *father*, who is an obvious allusion to God. It's not so much the *licentiousness* of the son but the *love* of the father that's in view. It isn't the nature of *man*, but of *God*, that concerns Jesus as He tells the story. The *son's conviction of sin* is important, but not as much as the *father's compassion*.

The parable is principally about the love of God the Father for His wayward and rebellious children. The story isn't about your sin or my sin. *It's about the Father's love for us in spite of our sin.* It's about the patience of a compassionate God who waits with open arms for us to come home. Virtually everything in the parable points to the extraordinary lengths to which the father goes to endure the worst of insults, all for the love of his child.

For example, today we think little of a son's request for his inheritance prior to his father's death. But it was unheard of in ancient Jewish culture. For fifteen years Kenneth Bailey asked people of the Middle East, from Morocco to India, from Turkey to the Sudan, about the implications of the son's request. The answers he got were consistent:

"Has anyone ever made such a request in your village?"

"Never!" came the reply.

"Could anyone ever make such a request?"

"Impossible!"

"If anyone ever did, what would happen?"

"His father would beat him, of course!"

"Why?"

"Because this request means he wants his father to die."[3]

There simply is no law or custom among the Jews or Arabs that entitles a son to a share of his father's wealth while the father is still in good health. On occasion a father might take the initiative himself and dispense his estate to his children. But *never* does the son make such a request. Far less does he demand that he also be given full right to dispose of the wealth as he sees fit. One can hardly imagine a more derisive insult to one's parent.

Thus we are led to expect a quick and punitive rebuke of the young man. But the father says nothing! This is the first of several instances where the father, impelled by compassion, breaks with custom. We see, then, that the emphasis is not so much on what the son's sin leads him to do as it is on what the father's love prompts him to endure.

The father is expected by custom and community to refuse the request and to discipline his son severely. Instead, in an unprecedented display of patient love, he grants his wish.

We are all quite familiar with the son's depraved fling in a faraway land. "Wine, women, and song" no doubt filled both his days and nights. The details of how he squandered his inheritance are left to the imagination of the reader. You fill in the blanks.

After reaching the end of his resources and finding himself living a pig's life, he concocts a plan to seek a place among his father's servants. After all, at his state *anything* would be an improvement.

The father may have assumed that his son had died. He knows that if he *is* alive, he's in for a rude reception upon his return home. The mockery, taunting, rejection, and perhaps even physical abuse that await him no doubt weigh heavily on the father's heart. We must therefore interpret what the father does next as a series of dramatic acts of compassionate self-sacrifice, all designed to protect his son from the harm and hostility of the community.

I'm only guessing, but I strongly suspect the father spent time each day with his eyes fixed on the horizon for any sign of his son's return. Each day he returned home more grieved than the day before. Each day the people of the community marveled at the patience of his love.

When the son finally returned, the father did what no one in his position would ever consider doing: He *ran* to meet him. Men of nobility and dignity never ran. Such behavior was humiliating and socially unacceptable. But this father didn't care. His only concern is to reach his son with protective love before an angry mob can get their hands on him.

Whatever inhibitions the father may have felt were drowned in the flood of affection for his child. Love for his son overshadows all concern for the opinion of others. Social etiquette will just have to suffer. All this father can think of is the joy of once again embracing his boy.

How would you have reacted had you been the father? Phil Davis reminds us that:

> A lesser parent would have waited for the son to arrive. He would have held back and expected his son to come and find him in the barn or the field. A lesser father would have appeared a bit stoic and unmoved. He would have perhaps not even lifted his eyes to meet the son, but instead would have shown his disapproval and hurt.
>
> A lesser father would have outlined the conditions of the son's return instead of laying out the red carpet unconditionally. He would have waited for an apology before showing acceptance, and may not have warmed up until his son showed some real signs of change. A lesser father would have made it clear that the son had to prove himself worthy again.
>
> A lesser father would have wanted some explanations: "Where did all the money go?" "Why did you act so foolishly?" A lesser father would have given a speech instead of a party. He would have given the son a red-faced stare instead of the red robe of honor and made the son feel guilty instead of special.[4]

But, then, we're not dealing here with an average dad. This man is acting the part of God. The love he displays is distinctly divine.

Under any other circumstances the son might have been embarrassed by his father's effusive love and PDA ("public display of affection"). But knowing what he did of the custom in that day, and expecting strict and exacting justice from the man whose name he had so callously degraded, he is obviously shattered by his father's love. Anticipating the worst, he is given the best, and it overwhelms him.

The father kisses him repeatedly, a sign of reconciliation and forgiveness. He adorns him with his own best robe, the one reserved for feast days and grand occasions. This is to ensure his acceptance by the community. The ring is an expression of trust, and the sandals were a sign of his being a free man (not a servant as he had planned) in his father's house. The calf, fed and fattened for extraordinary celebrations, is slaughtered and prepared for the biggest party that village had ever known.

Not surprisingly, given what we've seen of him to this point, the father's love is equally expressed toward the ungrateful older brother. In the first place, he should have immediately entered into the feast and participated in the joy of a repentant and restored brother. That he didn't was an insult to his father who was throwing the party.

Once again ancient custom anticipated the father's publicly rebuking and punishing him. By now, though, we've come to expect something different from this man. As with his younger, wayward son, he humbles himself and demonstrates self-effacing love. Look closely at the disgraceful way the older son treats his father.

- He refuses to address his father with the appropriate title of respect.
- He approaches his father not as a son but like a common laborer disputing his wages: "All these years I've been slaving for you and never disobeyed your orders!"
- He insulted his father in public yet has the gall to claim that he never disobeyed him!
- He accuses his father of playing favorites, complaining that he never got so much as a goat with which to party with his pals.
- He refuses to acknowledge the prodigal as his brother, referring to him contemptuously as "this son of yours" (v. 30).

It's possible that his demand for money sufficient to throw a banquet of his own is tantamount to his brother's sin of requesting the right to dispose of his inheritance. If so, the parable comes full circle with the older brother repeating his younger brother's offense of, in effect, desiring his father's death!

Yet through it all the father remains patiently loving. He reminds the older brother that his rights are fully protected. The return of the prodigal in no way affects his own inheritance.

At every turn the father's response is undeserved, unexpected, and unthinkable. But let me remind you that the love this father had for his two undeserving, indeed, *ill*-deserving, sons is a pale reflection of the love God has for you and me.

"But, Sam, you have no idea of the things I've done! Words can't begin to express how sinful I've been." Perhaps. But could it be worse than the actions of the prodigal? Could you have been more insolent and ungrateful than his older brother? Even if your rebellion makes these siblings look like cherubs, God's love is sufficiently patient to wait for your repentant return!

THE LESSONS OF LOVE

HEAR ME WELL. There is no sin, however deep or dark, that can repel, deter, or in any way diminish God's love for His children. We mistakenly think God loves us only so long as we remain loveable. When we fail, God's love falters. When we fall, God's love fades like a distant memory. No!

I'm not suggesting that God isn't grieved when we sin. His heart breaks when He sees His children return to the pit of sin. And as we shall see in the next chapter, He is diligent to apply disciplinary measures to bring them back. But His love never misses a beat. His love patiently waits.

I learned this lesson for myself back in the summer of 1970. I grew up in the turmoil of the sixties, entering the University of Oklahoma in 1969 at the height of civil unrest over the Vietnam War. It was the time for hippies, psychedelic drugs, and defiance of traditional authority. During that summer vacation I lived in Lake Tahoe, Nevada, and worked with a Christian group doing street evangelism. One thing I *didn't* do that summer was get a haircut. I distinctly recall rationalizing it by appealing to the fact that God looked on the inner man, not one's outer appearance. True enough, but I had failed to consider the message my long, blonde tresses were sending to my father.

I don't want to be misunderstood. Today the length of one's hair is a minor point and a personal preference that bears little if any spiritual significance. However, in 1970 long hair was more than mere fashion. It communicated a *social* message, one that my father vigorously opposed.

My father, now with the Lord, was a godly Christian man. He was also quite traditional and conservative, both theologically and politically. To him long hair was emblematic of everything he saw wrong in the United States. To him it was linked with opposition to the war, indulgence in drugs, and a repudiation of the structures of authority that he so dearly cherished and respected (i.e., the church, the state, and the family).

When I returned home unshorn and unshaven, it broke his heart. He thought (mistakenly) that he had lost his son. He was fearful that I had abandoned the values of my youth and had turned against those principles he had worked so hard to instill in me for nineteen years. I hadn't, but I now understand how he could have felt that way.

But he still loved me! His love never waned. He was grieved by my immaturity and the naive attempt to assert my individuality in a way that communicated more than I intended. But he was there to receive me back home. He never once considered locking me out. His love was strong enough to embrace his son in spite of my sin. That's what God's love for you is like. Although His heart breaks, it still beats. Grief doesn't destroy God's love. God grieves *because* He loves.

Is God's Love Unconditional?

AT THIS POINT someone will usually ask if this means God's love is *unconditional.* I'm not trying to be evasive, but *yes* and *no!*

In one sense God's love for you is unequivocally unconditional, for it in no way depends upon your personal loveliness. God doesn't suspend His love for you on the condition that you first prove loveable (or get a haircut). There are no antecedent conditions you must meet to induce God to show you favor.

But this doesn't mean that God is content to leave us in the moral state in which His love first found us. God is ruthlessly determined to rid us of our sin. Since genuine love always seeks the highest good of the beloved, God could never blink at the rebellion of His children or pretend it doesn't occur. He is relentless in the pursuit of purity in the hearts of those He loves.

"But, Sam, I'm so afraid of going to the well of God's love once too often and finding it empty." You can no more exhaust God's love than you can exhaust God! The well of God's forgiveness will dry up when God Himself dies. *As long as God lives, God loves.*

"But, Sam, I'm not good enough to be loved by God like that." Well of course you're not! I agree. Neither am I. That's what makes God's love for us so astounding.

If the prodigal son had been kind and generous and worthy and obedient, who would ever have thought much of the father's love for him? That kind of son is easy to love.

If you thought you were good enough to be loved of God, you wouldn't want His love or feel that you needed it. The only way to appreciate the love of God is to reach that point of self-awareness wherein you confess that there is nothing of which you are *less* worthy. Then God has you right where He wants. Then you are primed and poised on the brink of experiencing the kind of love the prodigal received as he looked up that dusty road and saw his daddy running to embrace him . . . with a song on his lips, I'm sure.

How long have you been away from "home?" Have you stayed away because you thought your sins had carried you beyond the point of no return? Perhaps you suspect that upon your return the "Christian" community might judge you or embarrass you or coldly turn its back.

Listen to me. I believe that if you were God's child when you left for that "faraway land" you are *still* God's child. If he was your Father then, He is your Father now. He stands waiting for you, patiently loving you.

If you listen closely enough you might even hear Him singing.

8

When Love Hurts

*P*AIN-FREE CHRISTIANITY. Sounds good, doesn't it? I can't think of anything more alluring than the prospect of the Christian life as a pleasant little jaunt down the yellow brick road on our way to some heavenly "Oz."

The problem is, although it sounds good, pain-free Christianity is a contradiction in terms. It doesn't exist, except in the deceptive sermons of some advocates of the health-and-wealth gospel!

If you want to be told that living for Jesus holds forth the potential for ease, comfort, and opulence, there is no shortage of those who will be only too happy to oblige you. They live for the opportunity to tickle your ears with promises of no sickness or suffering for those in whom there is no sin.

The appeal of this false gospel is self-evident. Who wouldn't want the best of everything with no discomfort, no disabilities, no distress? After all, we're not masochists! It really doesn't surprise me, therefore, that people should continue to ask, "If God loves me like you say, why do I hurt?" You may be a bit confused at this point in the book, wondering why this "singing God" doesn't seem to care more about your pain, your problems, your trials, and tribulations.

The reason is that *sometimes love hurts.* I don't mean that it hurts because we love someone who fails to love us back. I'm talking about God's love. Sometimes, because God is love, you will hurt.

I know this may sound out of sync with everything I've said so far, but it isn't. I'm not reneging on what I've already affirmed, namely, that God's love ushers you into the experience of indescribable joy, peace, freedom, and satisfaction. But on occasion we hurt and weep and are perplexed precisely *because* God is love.

Don't feel all alone if you're struggling to digest what I'm saying. There were quite a few Jewish Christians in the first century who couldn't make sense of their own suffering. Although they were well taught and intimately familiar with the Old Testament scriptures, these believers had forgotten what Solomon had said about suffering in Proverbs 3:11–12. So the author of the epistle to the Hebrews reminds them:

> And you have forgotten that word of encouragement that addresses you as sons: "My son, do not make light of the Lord's discipline, and do not lose heart when he rebukes you, because the Lord disciplines those he loves, and he punishes everyone he accepts as a son."
>
> Endure hardship as discipline; God is treating you as sons. For what son is not disciplined by his father? If you are not disciplined (and everyone undergoes discipline), then you are illegitimate children and not true sons. Moreover, we have all had human fathers who disciplined us and we respected them for it. How much more should we submit to the Father of our spirits and live! Our fathers disciplined us for a little while as they thought best; but God disciplines us for our good, that we may share in his holiness. No discipline seems pleasant at the time, but painful. Later on, however, it produces a harvest of righteousness and peace for those who have been trained by it.
>
> —HEBREWS 12:5–11

This passage of Scripture always seems to provoke discussion and debate. But I want to avoid that and direct your attention to three crucial truths contained in it. Make no mistake: If you ignore what God is saying to you in this text you will *never* fully appreciate and enjoy His love.

PAIN—THE PROOF OF SONSHIP

THE PAIN OF divine discipline is the proof of your Father's passionate love. This runs so counter to the mind of modern man that you may need to read it again, then put the Word down and let it slowly sink in. Contrary to what many child psychologists, and not a few theologians, have argued, "Discipline is the mark not of a harsh and heartless father but of a father who is deeply and lovingly concerned for the well-being of his son."[1]

"If I am God's child, why does He allow me to suffer?" is an absurd and inappropriate question. It is *because* you are His child, dear and precious to His heart, that He cleanses and educates you with various trials.

Before we go any further, perhaps it would be wise of me to state my position on a closely related and controversial subject. I believe in divine healing. I believe that God's love for us can be expressed in His decision to grant bodily healing, either in part or in whole, of both organic and functional physical maladies. Whether or not God chooses to heal us rests on His decision, not our demands.

In our church we pray regularly for the sick. We lay hands on those who are afflicted, we anoint them with oil in the name of the Lord, and we ask that God's healing touch restore them to full and robust health.

We have seen several people miraculously healed as a result. We have seen others die. But we will continue to pray both expectantly and submissively, because that is what God tells us to do (James 5:13–18).

I also believe that physical suffering and pain can serve a redemptive and sanctifying purpose in our lives. The lessons we learn in times of discomfort are many. Malcolm Muggeridge went so far as to say that virtually everything that truly enhanced and enlightened his existence came during times of affliction. He believed that "if it were possible to eliminate affliction from our earthly existence by means of some drug or other medical mumbo-jumbo, as Aldous Huxley envisaged in *Brave New World*, the result would not be to make life delectable, but to make it too banal and trivial to be endured."[2]

So how should you and I respond to physical ills? Without intending to be simplistic, let me suggest these steps.

If you are sick, ask the Lord to reveal to you if it is due to some sin in your life. If it is, confess and repent. Then pray that He would heal you. If it is not due to some specific transgression, still pray for healing. If He restores your health, give Him all the praise and honor. If He does not, continue to pray until such time as He either heals you or tells you to stop praying!

At all times, regardless of God's decision, submit to His loving and sovereign will and learn the lessons of life that He is attempting to teach.

Having said that about healing, I should point out that the discipline in view in Hebrews 12 is in all likelihood provoked by our sin. When we wander, when we stray, our loving Father chastens us, whether with physical distress, trials, or other forms of pain.

Far from a sign of God's hatred or indifference toward us, His love demands it!

To sin with impunity may at first strike you as attractive until you realize that it serves only to reveal that you are still a spiritual orphan. *If* you are God's child, you *will* receive His discipline. *If* God loves you, chastening is inevitable.

A friend of mine whom I'll call Steve commented one day on how harsh his father had been when Steve and his sister were growing up. That in itself didn't bother him so much as did the fact that his best friend seemed always to get away with murder! When their two families vacationed together, Steve and his sister consistently suffered consequences for their youthful mis-adventures, while their equally guilty friend was virtually ignored by his father.

At the time Steve was envious of his friend. He has since come to see that his own father's strict discipline was born not of cruelty but of concern for Steve's character. What appeared then to be the ideal parent was in fact the tragic expression of loveless and indifferent neglect.

I wouldn't say this if it weren't for the fact that the author of Hebrews says it. So here goes. To go through life pain-free, void of discipline, is to be a spiritual bastard. (See Hebrews 12:8.) A life free of hardship signals that you are no child of God. Rejoice, therefore, in your distress, for it proves you have a Father who cares enough to chasten.

There is one more point to make before moving on. Whereas it is true that the discipline in view *here* is provoked by disobedience, that isn't always the case. There are lessons in the Christian life that cannot be learned apart from a rigorous and often painful process.

God's love does not always provide us with a quick fix or an easy out. It isn't for lack of love that we are frequently left to struggle and fall and suffer both physical and spiritual injury. Sometimes love requires it.

Paul learned this from his thorn in the flesh. However you choose to interpret the thorn, one thing is clear: His discomfort was essential to his holiness. He wasn't being punished because of his sin. Rather, the thorn was God's device for keeping him from sin: "To *keep me from becoming* conceited . . . there was given me a thorn in my flesh" (2 Cor. 12:7, emphasis added).

J. I. Packer encourages us to think of this in terms of the training of children. He points out what every parent certainly knows, namely, that if "there are never any difficult situations that demand self-denial and discipline, if there are never any sustained pressures to cope with, if there are never any long-term strategies where the child must stick with an educational process, or an apprenticeship, or the practice of a skill for many years in order to advance, there will never be any maturity of character."[3]

Our kids may beg to differ. But if we cater to their demands in this regard they will grow up soft and spoiled, because everything will have been made too easy for them. Our heavenly

Father, on the other hand, will never allow that to happen in the lives of *His* children.

PERFECT PAIN

GOD'S DISCIPLINE IS always pure and perfect. It isn't always understandable, but it never misses the mark.

My earthly father is now with my heavenly Father. (I suspect they're having a great time together.) He was not only my father; he was my best friend. Our relationship was very special, and I miss him dearly.

One thing about my father, to which my sister will also testify, is that he was a firm disciplinarian. Like most godly parents, prior to the moment of truth (and pain), he would say something like, "Sam, this is going to hurt me more than it hurts you."

I never said so, but I distinctly remember thinking, *Who does he think he's kidding? It's* my *bottom that's getting whacked!* Being the father of two daughters myself, I now know what he meant.

The author of Hebrews says that "our fathers disciplined us for a little while as they thought best; but God disciplines us for our good, that we may share in his holiness" (12:10). My dad did what he "thought best."

But unlike God, his discipline wasn't perfect. If he were here he might want to argue that point, but I am convinced he erred on at least one occasion.

It happened one night during dinner. I couldn't have been more than six or seven years old. My mother had the audacity(!) to serve squash that night. I hate squash. I detest and loathe squash.

When God pronounced the curse on Adam, He said, "Cursed is the ground because of you; through painful toil you will eat squash all the days of your life. It will produce thorns and thistles for you, and you will eat the plants of the field [again, squash, I'm sure]. By the sweat of your brow you will eat squash" (Gen. 3:17–19, author's paraphrase).

I don't care how you fix it or in what other food you try to hide it; squash stinks. It is the curse of God that has befallen earth for Adam's sin. We are all being punished.

Several years ago Ann and I were invited to a dinner party at the home of some people from our church. I've always done my best to be a grateful guest, so when the host served squash that night I swallowed hard, sucked in my gut, asked God to forgive her, and ate the horrid stuff.

After each bite I quickly drank some iced tea, hoping to wash away the taste before it sent me into uncontrollable convulsions. But it didn't work. I couldn't figure it out, but no matter how much tea I drank, the taste of the squash only intensified.

My glass was soon empty. The host quickly retreated to the kitchen and returned with a pitcher of tea. I couldn't believe my eyes. There in the tea was a large slice . . . of squash! She was serving, of all things, *squash tea!* Never before nor since that fateful night have I heard of anyone serving squash tea!

This is a true story, so I hope and pray that if the hostess from that evening is reading this book, she won't mind my telling about the agony she unwittingly inflicted on me.

On second thought, anyone who would put squash on a plate *and* in tea deserves to be embarrassed!

Getting back to the point, though, I refused to eat squash the night my mother served it. My dad tried to persuade me that it was most certainly in my best interests if I did. I refused. He took decisive and disciplinary action. Ouch!

I have nothing but the highest regard and respect for my dad. But this time he blew it. To spank a child for refusing to eat squash is simply indefensible! Right?

Well, whatever you may think about squash, I can assure you that our heavenly Father *never* disciplines inappropriately. His chastisement of us is always perfect and just and timely. Though we may not always understand what He does, we can rest assured that He does it out of boundless love for His children.

We need never wonder or worry about the intent behind our distress. God is always seeking our best. He is neither too harsh nor too lenient. His chastening touch is perfectly suited to the need of our souls. If we chafe under His mighty hand it is *our* fault, not His.

PROFITABLE PAIN

THE FINAL LESSON to learn about God's chastening love is that although painful, it is always profitable.

"No discipline seems pleasant at the time, but painful," says our author. "Later on, however, it produces a harvest of righteousness and peace for those who have been trained by it" (Heb. 12:11).

In other words, pain *hurts*—but it's also *helpful*. God doesn't expect us to grit our teeth and deny that trials are troublesome. He knows the discomfort we feel in body and soul. He also knows that occasionally there simply is no other, or at least no better, way of cultivating holiness in the stubborn soil of our souls.

The next time you're hurting and tempted to question God's love for you, recall this verse. Remind yourself that the measure of true love is the pursuit of righteousness in the one loved. God permits us to hurt because He is passionately committed to making us holy. There is no love in providing comfort to someone in sin.

I'm assuming that if you were suffering from a recurring pain in your head, you would seek the advice and assistance of your family physician. Suppose he suggested that a couple of aspirin would suffice to eliminate the pain, knowing that its cause was in fact a malignant tumor? Your outrage would be wholly justified.

But what if he responded by saying, "I wanted to tell you the truth, but I knew how sad it would make you feel. I knew how painful it would be for you to undergo the required operation. I knew how much of an inconvenience and financial expense it would prove to be, so I thought it would be more loving if I wrote it off as just another headache."

My guess is that, notwithstanding his expression of love, you would be seriously tempted to sue for malpractice. If this doctor really cared for you he would have taken whatever steps necessary to preserve your life, even if those steps proved painful. Likewise our Father often has to perform a little spiritual surgery to excise the tumor of sin and rebellion and unbelief. It hurts; it's confusing. It's inconvenient, but above all else, it's loving.

When we're hurting, it's difficult to hear what anyone has to say, much less sing. But give it a try. The next time you feel the

and wi...
I'll strengthen th...
and cause thee to stand,
Upheld by My righteous,
omnipotent hand.
When through fiery trials
thy pathway shall lie,
My grace, all sufficient,
shall be thy supply.
The flame shall not hurt thee;
I only design
thy dross to consume
and thy gold to refine.[4]

9

Singing in a Cesspool

WHEN WE MOVED from Dallas, Texas, to Ardmore, Oklahoma, we were able to purchase a very old, but nicely remodeled, two-story home. It was nearly twice the square footage of our previous house and provided our then seven-year-old daughter, Melanie, with more than enough room to roam.

One night I let Melanie talk me in to playing "hide-and-go-seek." We used to play it in our much smaller Dallas home quite frequently, where it didn't prove to be much of a challenge. There were few places to hide and the game usually ended quickly. But now things were different. We switched off most of the lights, and I hid in what turned out to be the perfect spot. I could hear Melanie excitedly opening doors and looking behind furniture, but failing to find me. After a while the house grew silent. Not knowing if she were still looking or had given up, I emerged from my hideout and went downstairs.

I found her in the den, curled up on the couch, crying. When she saw me she leaped into my arms and squeezed me as if her life depended on it. "What's the matter, honey?" I asked, some-what confused. Shaking and sobbing, she said, "I was all alone in the dark and couldn't find you anywhere! I was scared!"

I strongly suspect that there are times when that's exactly how you feel in your relationship with God. It seems as if He's hiding from you, and no matter where or how long you search, He's not there. You're all alone in the dark and God isn't any-where to be found.

Some people call it depression. For others it seems more like hopelessness. Whatever name you put on it, the feeling is unmis-takable: God isn't there when you need Him most. His love is hidden somewhere in the dark and can't be found or felt.

It may be that you are feeling this right now. It may even be the reason you picked up this book, hoping to recover the sense of God's loving presence in your life. You try to convince yourself intellectually that God loves you. You memorize all the right Bible verses. You rehearse over and again the pastor's sermon on John 3:16. But you still feel all alone in the dark and can't find God anywhere. If God was just playing "hide-and-seek" with you He seems to have gotten bored and gone away. The courage you used to feel, knowing He was behind you, has vanished. The confidence to face anything life might throw in your path has given way to the horrifying suspicion that God has forgotten who and where you are.

Far from being able to hear God sing, you struggle just to remember the last time He spoke to you. Where is He now when you need Him most? Where is He when your life is enveloped in darkness and you can't find the light switch?

DARK NIGHT OF THE SOUL

DAVID, KING OVER ISRAEL, was no stranger to what you're feeling. Listen to his anguished cry. Perhaps you may find in him a soul mate.

> How long, O LORD? Will you forget me forever? How long
> will you hide your face from me? How long must I wrestle

with my thoughts and every day have sorrow in my heart?
How long will my enemy triumph over me? Look on me
and answer, O LORD my God. Give light to my eyes, or I
will sleep in death; my enemy will say, "I have overcome
him," and my foes will rejoice when I fall.

—PSALM 13:1–4

Although it's painful to read of someone suffering like this,
I'm also encouraged by it. It tells me that the Bible is going to
deal with me where I live, that I don't have to pretend everything
is okay when it's not. I find hope in the fact that "there is no
attempt in Scripture to whitewash the anguish of God's people
when they undergo suffering. They argue with God, they
complain to God, they weep before God. Theirs is not a faith
that leads to dry-eyed stoicism, but a faith so robust it wrestles
with God."[1]

Is life a bother for you right now? Is it a burden? Is there an
ache in your soul that won't go away? When you look up do you
see hovering overhead that same depressing dark cloud that
dogged your every step yesterday, and the day before, and the day
before that? Has it gotten to the point that when someone like
me comes along and says, "God loves you," your first instinct is
to punch 'em right in the nose?

"God loves me? You've got to be kidding! If He loves me so
much, why won't this pain go away? If He loves me like you say,
why am I all alone? He couldn't care less! And here I am, trying
to believe, and all my enemies make fun of my faith in a God
who seems to have forgotten where He left me!"

Sound familiar? Perhaps painfully familiar? What are we
supposed to do when God and His love seem hidden, and we're left
all alone? David has some words of insight and encouragement.

A CRY OF PAIN

FOUR TIMES DAVID cries out, "How long, O LORD?" *Four times!*
Don't just read the words. Listen to the confusion behind them.
"O Lord, will it *ever* end?"

It's important to note that David's feeling of abandonment is not related to some sin he's committed. We read of no confession, no contrition, no acknowledgment of personal guilt, no repentance that might shed some light on why God's blessings are missing. This isn't to say David was perfect. But at least in this case the cause for his turmoil must be traced to something other than overt transgression.

As with David, there are going to be down times in your life that are unrelated to specific acts of sin. Unfortunately this makes it even more difficult to handle! If you had sinned you could understand and live with God's absence, knowing you deserved to be chastised. But when God seems to disappear for no apparent reason the perplexity is unbearable.

David feels as if God has forgotten him. Has He? "Can the God of knowledge have a memory block? Can the only wise God be absent-minded? Is it possible that the Omniscient can forget, even for a moment, one of His children?"[2]

David is convinced He can. David is convinced He has! And he's frightened that God's forgetfulness might last forever.

But this was David's mistake. We must never permit our feelings to be the standard by which we measure biblical fact. God had most certainly *not* forgotten him, nor you.

Monday morning can be a pretty hectic time in our house. Typically it goes something like this: Joanna has misplaced the red hairbrush and has forgotten where it is. Melanie can't remember where she put her earrings. Ann is frantically searching for her car keys. And one of my shoes is missing! Turmoil reigns because everyone has forgotten where they put something.

Can God misplace one of His own children? Can God get so busy running the world and keeping the stars in space that He fails to remember our pain and our need? In all the complexities of life and the bustle of each day, can a Christian "slip God's mind?"

David surely thought so. He felt as though God had hidden His face from him. Since the "shining" or "showing" of God's face signifies blessing and favor (cf. Num. 6:24–26; Ps. 4:6; 31:16; 67:1; 80:3), for His face to be "hidden" is to suffer His withdrawal.

Not long ago I was speaking with a friend who had been rudely and unjustly dismissed from the pastorate of his church. Several families left the church with him and began a new ministry in the same town. He was describing to me how badly it hurt when so many of his former flock went out of their way to avoid contact with him. "For months," he said, "they wouldn't even look me in the face."

That's exactly how David feels. But in his case it's worse. Here it is *God* who David believes has turned His face away. "My heart says of you, 'Seek his face!' Your face, LORD, I will seek. Do not hide your face from me, do not turn your servant away in anger; you have been my helper. Do not reject me or forsake me, O God my Savior" (Ps. 27:8–9).

David lies awake at night "wrestling" with his thoughts, searching his mind for some explanation of God's absence. But to no avail. "All the while, like slow, circling vultures, his enemies hover above, waiting for his fall—and their meal!"[3]

David was by no means the only one of God's people to feel forgotten and abandoned. Consider Moses. The first forty years of his life were anything but boring. He had been raised and educated in the palace of Pharaoh. He had access to all the power, prestige, wealth, entertainment, and education that the greatest monarch on earth could provide. But it didn't last.

The next forty years were of a different order. After killing an Egyptian, he fled to Midian to save his skin (Exod. 2:11–15). For the next four decades he toiled in utter obscurity, tending the sheep and goats of Jethro, his father-in-law. Day after day, week after week, month after month, year after year, sheep and goats, goats and sheep, for forty long, tedious, quiet, boring years.

Gone? Yes. Forgotten? No. Simply because one of God's own is for the moment unused does not mean he is unloved. J. I. Packer tells us that "one of the disciplines to which the Lord calls us is the willingness, from time to time, *not* to be used in significant ministry."[4]

It may seem as if God has forgotten us. It may seem as if we've been interminably shelved (no doubt Moses thought this of himself). But not so.

Packer gives us an example to consider.

> Imagine, now, a devoted and gifted Christian woman,
> whose ministry has been precious to her, finding that for
> quite a long period the Lord sidelines her so that her poten-
> tial is not being used. What is going on? Is this spiritual
> failure? It is probably not spiritual failure at all, but a lesson
> in Christ's school of holiness. The Lord is reminding her
> that her life does not depend on finding that people need
> her. *The prime source of her joy must always be the knowledge of
> God's love for her*—the knowledge that though He did not
> need her, He has chosen to love her freely and gloriously so
> that she may have the eternal joy of fellowship with Him.
> Regarding her ministry, what matters is that she should be
> available to Him. Then He will decide when and how to
> put her to service again, and she should leave that with Him
> (emphasis added).[5]

God hadn't forgotten this lady. He hadn't abandoned Moses
or David. Nor has He forsaken you.

A CRY OF PRAYER

SUDDENLY, THOUGH, when all seems lost, David breaks forth in
prayer. But why? If it is really true that God has turned away,
why pray to Him? If God has forgotten, why bother? Yet David
does pray. He can't help but cry out to the God that, deep down,
he knows is still there, loving him.

"Look on me and answer, O LORD my God. Give light to my
eyes, or I will sleep in death" (Ps.13:3). I doubt that David is
talking about physical death. Literally it reads to "sleep the sleep
of death," a reference most likely to depression or some form of
spiritual anguish.

Despair can often be seen in someone's face. Their voice may
sound okay, but their eyes betray them. My father was often able
to discern if either I or my sister was sick simply by looking into
our eyes. If we didn't look well "in our eyes" we probably weren't.

Evidently David's emotional anguish was visibly noticeable. He requests that God would restore a spiritual sparkle to his eyes. "O God, make my eyes gleam with Your grace and mercy once again."

But more was at stake than just David's sense of well-being. God's reputation was on the line! David prays, "O LORD, don't give the enemy any excuse to blaspheme your name. Don't let them gloat over my condition and slander your name when they see the defeat of your servant." (See Psalm 13:4.)

A CRY OF PRAISE

SOMETIMES THE FRUSTRATIONS of the present threaten to undermine the trust that comes from remembering the past. We are so lost *now* that we forget what happened back *then*. "What good is yesterday when I'm hurting so badly today?"

That is where faith comes in. Faith in the God we've seen act in the past renews our hope for the future. David knew it. So he makes a choice, the same choice you and I must make. He decides to entrust himself to God's pledge of undying love. If you hear only one thing in the reading of this book, let it be the words of David in Psalm 13:5–6. Make them *your* words.

"But I trust in your unfailing love; my heart rejoices in your salvation. I will sing to the LORD, for he has been good to me" (emphasis added).

Yes, on occasion God does seem hidden from view. His presence feels like a fast-fading memory. His love seems to have evaporated under the hot summer sun. When that happens, do what David did. Take yourself in hand, and, contrary to every fiber of your being that demands you say otherwise, declare to the heavens: *"But I trust in Your unfailing love!"*

God's love will not fail! It has not nor will it die. Though hidden from view, though far from what you're feeling, God's love for you lives. Go ahead if you want and punch me right in the nose! I may stop loving you (for the moment), but God won't.

Observe how David resolves to rejoice in God's salvation (deliverance) even though it has not yet come. David is still depressed. It is as if he says, "O God, I am trusting in You to create the occasion when I can again look on Your acts of deliverance and rejoice in Your saving power." From what he recalls of God's faithfulness in the past, there arises in his heart the calm of anticipation. "O God, You did it once before. I am confident You will do it again, because Your love is unfailing!"

SINGING IN THE CESSPOOL

SOMEONE MIGHT OBJECT, insisting that it's one thing to resolve inwardly to cling to God's unfailing love, but something else to "sing" to the Lord as David did. Oh, really?

At a conference in Brighton, England, in 1991, a remarkable word of testimony was given by a pastor from China. He had spent eighteen years in a prison for his faith. Here is a man who seemed to have every reason to doubt God's love for him. But he didn't.

His assigned task in the camp was to empty the human waste cesspool. That's right. It's exactly what you think it is! Being atheists, the prison guards took sadistic pleasure in giving this job to the Christian pastor whose faith they despised. They never knew what a blessing it turned out to be! Listen as this remarkable man of God describes his experience:

> It was more than two metres in breadth and two metres in length, filled with human waste collected from the entire camp. Once it was full, the human waste was kept until it was ripe and then dug out and sent to the fields as fertilizer. Because the pit was so deep I could not reach the bottom to empty it; I had to walk into the disease-ridden mass and scoop out successive layers of human waste, all the time breathing the strong stench. The guards and all the prisoners kept a long way off because of the stench.
>
> So why did I enjoy working in the cesspool? I enjoyed the solitude. In the labour camp all the prisoners normally were under strict surveillance and no one could be alone. But when I worked in the cesspool I could be alone and could pray to our Lord as loudly as I needed. I could recite the Scriptures, including all the Psalms I still remembered,

and no one was close enough to protest. That's the reason I enjoyed working in the cesspool. Also I could sing loudly the hymns I still remembered.

In those days one of my most favourites was "In the Garden." Before I was arrested this was my favourite hymn, but at that time I did not realise the real meaning of this hymn. When I worked in the cesspool I knew and discovered a wonderful fellowship with our Lord. Again and again I sang this hymn and felt our Lord's presence with me.

> I come to the garden alone,
> While the dew is still on the roses;
> And the voice I hear, falling on my ear,
> The Son of God discloses.
> And He walks with me, and He talks with me,
> And He tells me I am his own;
> And the joy we share as we tarry there
> None other has ever known.[6]

Again and again as I sang this hymn in the cesspool, I experienced the Lord's presence. He never left me nor forsook me. And so I survived and the cesspool became my private garden.[7]

The next time you begin to wonder if God really loves you, try singing in your cesspool. God's love can work wonders virtually anywhere!

ETERNAL ENCOURAGEMENT

THE LONGER I reflect on this Chinese pastor's experience the more convinced I am of the truth of Paul's words in 2 Thessalonians 2:16. There he says that because of God's love for us we have been given "eternal encouragement." Not a momentary boost nor a temporary surge, but encouragement that is eternal, unending, ceaseless, both for now and in the ages to come!

What we must realize, however, is that encouragement from

the Lord sometimes will come in small doses. It's always there, but not always easy to discern at first glance. I discovered the truth of this only recently in what I consider a remarkable example of eternal encouragement.

It was a time of spiritual dryness. I was depressed, frustrated, and confused. Worst of all, God didn't seem to care. I was in hiding and so was He, or so I thought. Then something occurred that at first perplexed me.

I was having lunch with a man who, together with his wife and family, lives and ministers in Hong Kong. We had never met before that day. He had never visited our church and knew nothing about me or my ministry, past or present.

During the course of our two-hour conversation, we discussed a variety of different issues pertaining both to his work on the mission field and my pastorate. The surprising thing about it, though, was that through all of our conversation he mentioned two, and only two, texts of Scripture. I don't recall the context of his remarks or what provoked them, but he appealed to a passage in John 1, and then to another in Joshua 3.

So what? I'll tell you what! How many verses are there in the Bible? I don't know either, but there are probably several thousand. It "just so happened" that the two texts he mentioned were the very two on which I was scheduled to preach the following Sunday! He had no idea I was preaching on John 1 on Sunday morning and on Joshua 3 on Sunday night.

Now, you figure the odds. Was it merely coincidence? It wasn't as if he had quoted dozens of texts and included a reference to those two. They were the *only* two he mentioned. Ask an odds-maker what the chances are of this occurring. My guess is you would be more likely to win a state lottery than to select precisely the two texts on which I was to preach that week.

Why did this happen? I wrestled for days trying to discern some grand spiritual symbolism in what was an undeniably stunning incident. Then it came to me. I'm convinced beyond all doubt that this was an example of God's eternal encouragement during a time when His love was hidden from view. It was God's way of saying, "Sam, I'm still here. I still care. And contrary to what you're feeling right now, I am still in control."

I don't know why God chose this approach. Perhaps He did it this way to remove all doubt from my mind that it was *He* who was behind it all. You may think it trivial. You may even think I am blowing a mere happenstance completely out of proportion or reading more into a chance event than is actually there. Think what you want. But you're wrong.

What happened that day in that restaurant during that conversation with that missionary from Hong Kong was nothing less than a providential serendipity designed to encourage my disconsolate and disheartened soul. It worked!

I can't promise that God will do precisely that for you. But I can assure you that His love, though at times hidden, will supply for your soul just what is needed to sustain you through the most distressing of trials. It may be small, but it will be sufficient.

GOD AND FORGETFUL MOTHERS

IT'S HARD FOR most of us to imagine a mother abandoning her child. But it happens. Only recently police in Oklahoma City, Oklahoma, discovered a two-day-old infant in a dumpster behind an apartment complex. He was wrapped up in a garbage bag, disguised to look like just so much discarded trash. The mere thought of it challenges credulity and inflames our rage. It's rare, but it happens.

When I saw the report of this incident on the evening news, my mind turned to Isaiah 49:14–16:

> But Zion said, "The LORD has forsaken me, the Lord has forgotten me." Can a mother forget the baby at her breast and have no compassion on the child she has borne? Though she may forget, *I will not forget you!* See, I have engraved you on the palms of my hands (emphasis added).

Melanie was certain that I had forgotten her. She feared that I had left the house, abandoning her to the darkness. But I was only in hiding, for the moment. Her joy returned when she again saw my face and felt my embrace. God hasn't stopped loving you. You may not see Him. But He hasn't forgotten you.

When lingering storm clouds obscure the sun's rays, we begin to wonder: *Will I ever feel its warmth again?* Then we remind ourselves of the laws of nature and wait expectantly for the skies to break.

God's love for you always shines bright. But if clouds of pain and rejection and shame have for the moment blackened the sky, rest assured that gracious winds will again blow strong and the warmth of His passionate love will renew your once cold soul.

In anticipation, go ahead and sing like David did. Go ahead and sing like that pastor in the prison cesspool. Who knows, you just might hear God join you with a song of His own!

10

A Love You Can Count On

*M*IKE HAD TO confide in someone. He had tried, but he could no longer keep it to himself. He needed the strength that would come from the understanding and encouragement of another Christian man. So he told his story to his best friend, Joe.

It wasn't easy for Mike to open up and tell Joe about his struggle with homosexual temptations. But he trusted Joe. Besides, he needed someone to pray for him. He hadn't yet given in to his lusts but he felt himself weakening.

Joe promised he would preserve Mike's secret. He didn't. It wasn't long before it seemed as if everyone in town knew. Mike was devastated and enraged. A lifelong friendship shattered upon a confidence betrayed.

Karla can't remember how old she was when the abuse began. She had tried for so long to forget it, but like a submerged beach ball the painful memory refused to stay beneath the surface of her soul.

The anguish was intensified by the fact that her abuser was an uncle whom she adored. He treated her like a queen. He singled her out for special favors and was quick to defend her whenever anyone threatened her harm.

"How could someone I loved turn on me like that? I trusted him, and he took advantage of me. Are all men that way?"

Terry was as faithful as the proverbial hound dog. The thought of cheating on his wife never crossed his mind. He never dreamed it would cross hers to cheat on him.

Angela insists she didn't pursue the relationship. But at this point it made no difference to Terry. The damage had been done. After Angela confessed the affair, Terry withdrew into his shell. "If I can't count on Angela," he asked, teary-eyed, "whom *can* I count on?"

After Susan's husband died of a heart attack, she turned to the family accountant for financial advice. She had never been good with numbers. Her husband, Steve, had always taken care of everything. She didn't even know how much money they had.

When news broke that the accountant had been diverting money into his own pocket, Susan hit rock bottom. "How could anyone exploit the weakness of a widow and her three kids? What am I going to do now? I'm broke, and I'm all alone."

Four different people. Four different tragedies. Yet they all share one thing in common: They put their trust in someone who proved to be untrustworthy. They banked on the character of a friend and got burned. All four were betrayed. All four now find it next to impossible to trust anyone for anything. As a result, all four are profoundly miserable.

What are we supposed to do when our confidence craters? To whom do we turn when our closest friend has turned on us? These are not pleasant questions, especially when the answers aren't quick in coming.

Everyone, in one way or another, is suffering from a loss of confidence. People have lost confidence in the president. His approval rating is at an all-time low. We hear of a crisis in confidence concerning the government. Trust in the character and competency of our elected officials has been severely eroded. People don't think much of our educational system, and the economy scares the socks off most.

Here's the really bad news. When disillusioned husbands and wives sit in front of me and angrily declare they'll not love again until the one who betrayed them proves trustworthy, I'm forced to tell them that means they'll never love at all. The fact is, no one is trustworthy.

I'm not being cynical, just realistic. We are all sinners. No one, not even the most mature of Christians, can guarantee that he will always be there, never lie, forever keep a secret, and by no means ever stray.

If you are determined never again to love or give until some person becomes utterly trustworthy, you're doomed to a life of self-protective suspicion and other-destroying manipulation.

So what's a person to do? What's a *Christian* to do? If no one is infallibly worthy of our unquestioning trust, where do we turn? To whom do we ultimately look? In what do we put our hope?

You would have had to be reading with your eyes closed (how does one do that?) not to know where I'm leading you. The answer is obvious. The only thing in life or death that merits our trust is God's love. The dollar may rise or fall, nations may totter on the brink of destruction, health may improve or disintegrate, but through it all the confidence of the child of God ought to remain constant and unaffected, because God's love never fails.

Three times in Psalm 33 we are told about God's "unfailing love." Banks fail. Marriages fail. Friends fail. But God's love for you is unfailing. When everything and everyone else bottoms out, the psalmist assures us that "the earth is full of his [God's] *unfailing love*" (v. 5). The eyes of the Lord, he tells us, are "on those whose hope is in his *unfailing love*" (v. 18). His prayer gets right to the point: "May your *unfailing love* rest upon us, O LORD, even as we put our hope in you" (v. 22).

GOD IS LOVE

WE'RE ALL FAMILIAR with the statement in 1 John 4:8 that "God is love." This doesn't mean that there is nothing in God but love. Once you've said everything about the love of God you haven't said everything about God. The God who is love is equally holy and true and righteous and merciful and powerful.

Perhaps John means that "God is a lover." That sounds less clinical than "God is love." Love is what God *feels* and *does,* not just what God *is.* I have no problem with that.

Whatever the precise intent of John in saying God is love, at minimum he means that love is an eternal and essential attribute of God's being and doing. Therefore, God will never not love (pardon the double negative). God's love is unfailing because it is *God's* love. God's love will fail when God Himself does. As I said in an earlier chapter, so long as God lives, God loves.

Could anything be more worthy of our trust than that which always is? If God's love never fails, where better to place our faith? Unlike Mike's "friend," Karla's uncle, Terry's wife, and Susan's accountant, God's love does come with a guarantee.

Whatever else may happen in this world, whoever else may turn his back on you when the chips are down, of this you may be sure: She whose trust and hope and confidence is in the unfailing love of God will never be put to shame.

That's what Psalm 33 is all about. It was written to remind you and me that there is one refuge that is impenetrable to disappointment and betrayal. You may think you're all out of confidence, but what little you've got left, invest in the unfailing love of an undying God.

There are good reasons for that exhortation. The psalmist isn't just making noise or writing pretty poetry. There are some things he tells us about God Himself that make this act of trust eminently reasonable. Let's look at them.

GOD'S UNSTAINED PRINCIPLES

For the word of the LORD is right and true; he is faithful in all he does. The LORD loves righteousness and justice; the earth is full of his unfailing love.

—PSALM 33:4–5

Whatever God does is righteous because God does it. God

doesn't do righteous things because that is what righteousness requires. Righteousness is defined by who God is and by what He does. Not only that, but He *loves* righteousness. He doesn't just do it; He *delights* to do it!

When I hear God say, "Sam, I love you," I take refuge in the fact that "the word of the LORD is right and true." Others may loudly proclaim their affection for me. They may swear to their ultimate demise that nothing will diminish their commitment to my cause. I hope they're right. But I know God is, for "he is faithful in all he does."

GOD'S UNLIMITED POWER

> By the word of the LORD were the heavens made, their starry host by the breath of his mouth. He gathers the waters of the sea into jars; he puts the deep into storehouses. Let all the earth fear the LORD; let all the people of the world revere him. For he spoke, and it came to be; he commanded, and it stood firm.
>
> —PSALM 33:6–9

Like most parents, on occasion I talk myself blue in the face when dealing with my kids. For some strange reason I actually expect them to do immediately whatever I say. It doesn't always work out that way!

But God speaks and it is done! It is as easy (easier) for God to create everything out of nothing as it is for you to utter a word. Now that's the kind of God who inspires confidence! God says *Be!* and it is! God said *Light!* and light was! *Land!* and land was; *Flowers!* and flowers were; *Cows!* and the first moo was heard!

This God of power is the one in whose love we find refuge. An anonymous psalmist affirms for himself and us all that "he who dwells in the shelter of the Most High will rest in the shadow of the Almighty. I will say of the LORD, 'He is my refuge and my fortress, my God, in whom I trust'" (Ps. 91:1–2).

Not too far from the house in which I was raised in Shawnee, Oklahoma, there is an area called Broadway Woods. It would hardly classify as a forest, but to a nine-year-old boy it seemed as big and vast as the deepest, darkest jungles of Africa.

I loved playing in Broadway Woods. My friends and I would build little hideouts and secret meeting places there, using whatever materials we could scrounge up. We'd throw together a few pieces of discarded plywood, cover them over with tree branches, and make for ourselves a hidden clubhouse. All we wanted was a refuge from parents, big sisters, and older boys in the neighborhood who beat up on us. It was great.

That's what Psalm 91:1–2 is talking about: a secret hiding place, finding refuge and protection from enemies; dwelling in safety and security. But not in some poorly constructed shanty. Our spiritual fortress is God Himself! *He* is our hiding place. David says much the same thing in another psalm:

> How great is your goodness, which you have stored up for those who fear you, which you bestow in the sight of men on those who take refuge in you. In the shelter of your presence you hide them from the intrigues of men; in your dwelling you keep them safe from accusing tongues.
>
> —PSALM 31:19–20

And yet again:

> For you have been my refuge, a strong tower against the foe. I long to dwell in your tent forever and take refuge in the shelter of your wings.
>
> —PSALM 61:3–4

Try to envision God's power as forging His love into a strong and impregnable fortress. God doesn't build us a shanty out of leaves and rotting wood. God's *love* is our shelter. He Himself is our hiding place. His presence is our peace, our protection, our refuge.

Whom is this for? It is for the one who "dwells" in the shelter of the Most High. Do you live in God's presence every day, or do you merely visit Him for an hour on Sunday? The promised blessings of this psalm are not for those who occasionally run to God for help when they're in trouble. Nor is it for the sporadic, once-in-a-while pray-er. God is a refuge to those who habitually seek their abode in Him.

Let me return to Broadway Woods for a moment. Eventually, my friends and I would have to leave our fortress behind. The comfort of our tree house only lasted a short while. The time would come for us to emerge from the secrecy of our hideaway and reenter the real world.

But that never happens for those who seek shelter in the Most High. God is our permanent refuge in whom we abide while we are at work or at school or wherever. We never have to leave God and go home. He *is* our home. It is in Him and in His love that we move and live and have our being.

God's Unstoppable Purpose

> The LORD foils the plans of the nations; he thwarts the purposes of the peoples. But the plans of the LORD stand firm forever, the purposes of his heart through all generations. Blessed is the nation whose God is the LORD, the people he chose for his inheritance.
>
> —PSALM 33:10–12

> Many are the plans in a man's heart, but it is the LORD's purpose that prevails.
>
> —PROVERBS 19:21

> There is no wisdom, no insight, no plan that can succeed against the LORD. The horse is made ready for the day of battle, but victory rests with the LORD.
>
> —PROVERBS 21:30–31

> I make known the end from the beginning, from ancient times, what is still to come. I say: My purpose will stand, and I will do all that I please.
>
> —ISAIAH 46:10

Superpowers convene summit meetings and vast, multi-national corporations formulate their strategies, but it is the purpose of God that shall stand. Even your weekly "To-Do" agenda is incorporated into the accomplishment of God's purpose. Human plans and schemes are always subject to divine restraint.

Nothing is more futile than for people to oppose the purpose of God. Said Spurgeon, "Their persecutions, slanders, false-hoods, are like puff-balls flung against a granite wall."[1] The cause of God is never in danger. Even on that one occasion in history when it seemed God's design was in jeopardy, He had it all in hand.

> This man [Jesus] was handed over to you by God's set pur-pose and foreknowledge; and you, with the help of wicked men, put him to death by nailing him to the cross.
> —ACTS 2:23

In crucifying Jesus these men simply "did what your [God's] power and will had decided beforehand should happen" (Acts 4:28).

When Joni Eareckson Tada visited Oklahoma City, Oklahoma, to speak at a conference on disability and the church, she explained how her initial perspective on the diving "accident" that left her a quadriplegic had changed. At first she envisioned God turning His back momentarily to attend to some problem in a far-away land. Satan, seizing the moment, placed his foot in the small of her back and shoved her into the shallow waters of the Chesapeake Bay.

God, startled by her cry, whirls around . . . too late. He is left to piece back together the shattered remains of her life. No! And again she said, *no!*

Joni doesn't profess to understand all the intricacies of God's sovereignty, but neither is she free to dismiss Him from any role in her "accident." His ultimate purpose for her was not side-tracked by Satan's devices. He *can* be trusted, even when His purpose for us is not identical with ours.

GOD'S UNIVERSAL PRESCIENCE

> From heaven the LORD looks down and sees all mankind;
> from his dwelling place he watches all who live on earth—
> he who forms the hearts of all, who considers everything
> they do.
>
> —PSALM 33:13–15

For several years I was a season-ticket holder for all University of Oklahoma football games. I rarely missed one. The players at OU are often heard referring to the "Eye in the Sky," a camera strategically placed to record everything on the field. "The eye in the sky doesn't lie," so they say. But sometimes it does. Occasionally a player can get away with a missed tackle or a penalty. Every now and then he can hide.

But there is another "Eye in the Sky" that never misses so much as a heartbeat. Even your unspoken opinions about what you've been reading in this book are known by God before they are thought. As David said elsewhere, "The LORD is in his holy temple; the LORD is on his heavenly throne. He observes the sons of men; his eyes examine them" (Ps. 11:4).

God sees it all, simultaneously and wholly. From the North Pole to the South Pole, whether in Russia or the Rio Grande Valley, on hilltops and in river beds, in caves and in palaces.

GOD'S UNCHANGING PASSION

> No king is saved by the size of his army; no warrior escapes
> by his great strength. A horse is a vain hope for deliverance;
> despite all its great strength it cannot save. But the eyes of
> the LORD are on those who fear him, on those whose hope
> is in his unfailing love, to deliver them from death and keep
> them alive in famine. We wait in hope for the LORD; he is
> our help and our shield. In him our hearts rejoice, for we
> trust in his holy name. May your unfailing love rest upon
> us, O LORD, even as we put our hope in you.
>
> —PSALM 33:16–22

Why do our hearts fail from fear? Why is there a crisis in confidence? Because most are tempted to trust in human strength and to rely on earthly stratagems. Human power and human promises are notoriously tenuous. It isn't the army that ultimately saves the king nor the warrior that brings him victory.

So where must our confidence be placed? In whom or what must we place our hope? In God's *unfailing love!* To the Israelites only recently delivered from Egypt Moses said, "In your [God's] *unfailing love* you will lead the people you have redeemed" (Exod. 15:13, emphasis added).

And why does God not take pleasure in horses and chariots and the strength of men? Did He not make them all? Yes, but what displeases the Lord is those who *hope* in such earthly props. John Piper explains:

> He is displeased with people who put their hope, for example, in missiles or in makeup, in tanks or tanning parlors, in bombs or body-building. God takes no pleasure in corporate efficiency or balanced budgets or welfare systems or new vaccines or education or eloquence or artistic excellence or legal processes, when these things are the treasure in which we hope, or the achievement in which we boast. Why? Because when we put our hope in horses and legs, then horses and legs get the glory, not God.[2]

What is the anticipated response to all this?

OUR UNINHIBITED PRAISE

> Sing joyfully to the LORD, you righteous; it is fitting for the upright to praise him. Praise the LORD with the harp; make music to him on the ten-stringed lyre. Sing to him a new song; play skillfully, and shout for joy.
>
> —PSALM 33:1–3

What we now know about God and His unfailing love calls for loud and jubilant exultation, not because God is hard of hearing, but because the psalmist knows it is natural for men and women to rejoice loudly in that which they find most delightful.

We are to sing to God a "new song." Why? Because every time we gather to worship as the body of Christ we have new and fresh reasons to sing! "You'll never believe what God did for me yesterday!" "Oh, yes, I will. But first let me tell you what I learned about God's character from Romans!"

For some time now a commercial has appeared regularly on TV, promoting a certain alcoholic beverage. Good ol' boys are pictured sitting around a campfire or on the beach, guzzling their favorite beer, when one of them says, "Ya' know, it just doesn't get any better than this!"

The Christian can never say that! Not because there's a better drink that he hasn't yet tasted, but because with God there's always a fresh display of goodness and grace. Each day brings a new and more powerful manifestation of His greatness and mercy. God Himself creates the need for new songs by granting new insight into His works and ways. He is constantly doing new and fresh things for which we need new and fresh declarations in song!

A BLANKET OF LOVE

JEREMIAH DENTON SPENT eight years in a Vietnamese prison camp as a POW. He was released in 1973. Denton has a story that every Christian needs to hear. I can't tell it all here, but permit me to close with one incident that says a little about Denton and a lot about his God.

Denton was subjected to repeated torture during his stay in prison. In an interview,[3] he described an elaborate device that drove dull metal into his tendons and a bar that was manipulated into his leg. His hands were held fast by painfully sharp handcuffs called "hellcats."

For five days and nights Denton ate nothing and slept very little. After enduring repeated beatings, he sensed that he was close to death.

I'll let him tell what happened next:

One night I had been through all of the prayers that I could think of . . . It was at the end of a second set of five days of torture. I said to God, "Lord, I have no will, no means left with which to resist. You say, 'Ask and you shall receive.' I have asked; I haven't received. I am totally helpless. . . . So I am turning it all over to You. Everything. It is up to You to get me out of this or let me die here."

I was suffering a chill when I made that act of total self-surrender. The instant I finished that prayer—I stopped shaking; I didn't feel any pain. It was like a blanket, like warm air . . . something tangible that came over me . . . I wasn't cold any more. I felt zero pain. Zero anxiety. Zero fear.[4]

What happened? Only Jeremiah Denton knows for sure, but I'll venture a guess. I suggest that here is one man who had no choice but to put his trust in God's unfailing love. That's all he had left. No props, no power, no money to buy his way to freedom, or medicine to soothe his pain. Only God. And like a warm blanket, the love of the Father wrapped around the body and soul of Jeremiah Denton and brought him a warmth no words can describe.

Jeremiah Denton was still in prison though. But so was his God. And that was enough for this one POW to find the will to survive.

Can you trust me? Well, on at least one thing you can. Trust me when I say that you can always trust God's unfailing love. When all else fails, when all others fail, God will *still* be singing over you.

11

Love's Vice Grip!

I WAS COOKING hamburgers on a charcoal grill when it came to me. "Yeah! That's just the way most people think about God's love!" Let me explain what happened.

I'm not very patient when it comes to getting charcoal lit. I tend to get a bit frustrated after going through an entire book of matches and a can of lighter fluid. It wouldn't be so bad if the sack of charcoal hadn't promised that only one match and no fluid would do the trick. Don't believe everything you read.

If it weren't for our hungry friends, I'd have given up. But I wanted to be a good host. So I doused the briquettes with more fluid and threw a veritable blaze of matches on the pile (contrary to instructions and all common sense). Finally, a flicker of hope. The flame gradually increased and the coals grew white hot. The heat felt good. The burgers tasted great.

After a while, though, the fire died down. The coals became cold and the heat dissipated. All that was left was an ashen mess. We often tend to view God's love for us like the fire in my grill.

We have to work hard to get it going. Good deeds—or at least good intentions—tithing, church attendance, payment of our taxes, kindness, and other such efforts are pursued in hopes that they will ignite the fire of God's affection.

For a while it seems to work. We feel the warmth of His passion, see the glow of His smiling approval, and experience the blessings of His favor. Nothing tastes so sweet as the flavor of God's love.

But after a while, no matter how hard we try, His love for us grows cold. The flame dies out. The warmth of His presence disappears, and all that is left are the ashes of a messed-up life.

Is that how you think of God's love? Do you live as if His love for you were somehow dependent on your love for Him? Do you live in fear that someday it will all come to an end and you'll be left out in the cold, hungry and alone? Are you sick and tired of working to fan the flames of His love, desperately afraid that the fire of His affection will someday be extinguished?

I want to put your heart at rest. I want to convince you that your fears are unfounded, that they are a lie of the enemy who wants to fill you with crippling anxiety over the state of your soul. I want to demonstrate to you from Scripture, from *God's* own Word, that His love for His children will *never* die. I want you to know with unshakeable assurance that His love will preserve you safe and saved forever and ever.

THE MUCH-MORE LOVE OF GOD

YOU ARE PROBABLY quite familiar with Romans 5. You may even have memorized it. But I want us to look at it one more time. What you see may surprise you.

> You see, at just the right time, when we were still powerless, Christ died for the ungodly. Very rarely will anyone die for a righteous man, though for a good man someone might possibly dare to die. But God demonstrates his own love for us in this: While we were still sinners, Christ died for us.
> —ROMANS 5:6–8

When did Christ die? No, I don't mean at nine in the morning or three in the afternoon. Paul says Christ died "at just the right time," in due time, better still, in *God's* time. His death was no accident of history, nor quirk of fate. The Son died when the Father wanted Him to. It isn't something that slipped up on God's blind side or caught Him napping. Christ died "at just the *right* time."

For whom did Christ die? Paul provides a four-fold description.

Jesus died for *powerless* people, people "without strength" (KJV), *helpless* people (NAS), spiritually impotent people. Jesus died for people who were unable to prepare themselves for anything spiritual and unable to perform anything spiritual. He died for people who were powerless to do or think or say anything that might induce the Father to give His Son for them.

If God only helps those who help themselves, He's going to be more helpless than we. God helps those who are utterly and absolutely helpless.

Jesus also died for *ungodly* people. He didn't die for a single godly man or woman. He died for those who aren't simply unlike God but for people who are hostile toward Him. It isn't so much that we're different from God. We detest Him. Yet for such people He sent His Son to die!

It gets worse. Jesus also died for *sinners*. There aren't two classes of people in the world: godly people who don't sin and ungodly ones who do. All are ungodly sinners. For such Christ died.

Finally, He died for *enemies* (v. 10). Christ died for rebellious, insolent, haughty, arrogant, self-righteous, self-sufficient, repulsive, disobedient, at-war-with-God sinners.

Why do I stress this point? Because otherwise we will take God's love for granted. As long as we see ourselves as loveable His love will never grip our hearts as the astounding and incomprehensible thing that it is. We think of God's love and say, "Sure, it seems reasonable to me. Why shouldn't He love me? It makes perfectly rational and logical sense."

We think like this because we fancy ourselves not helpless but competent, not ungodly but godlike, not sinners but saints, not enemies but allies. The point is, we will never understand the love of God, which we don't deserve, until we understand the wrath of God, which we most assuredly deserve.

Note carefully Paul's argument. When he speaks of a "righteous" man and a "good" man, he is speaking in human terms. If you doubt this, see Romans 3:10.

The so-called "righteous" man is the one who fulfills his duty in life. He meets his obligations. He is lawful, but not necessarily gentle. He is firm, but not always friendly. Paul says that although we might respect someone like that, we probably wouldn't go so far as to die for him.

The "good" man, on the other hand, has the added qualities of kindness and compassion. He evokes our admiration and affection. For such a person you might be willing to die. The odds are a bit more in his favor than they are for the righteous man.

But look what God did! God demonstrated His love for us by sending His Son to die for powerless, ungodly, sinful, hostile men and women. Not the righteous, not the good, but the indescribably bad. What you and I would only reluctantly do for someone we consider "good," God joyfully and spontaneously did for people who are by all counts bad! God's love cuts across the grain of every known or implied rule of human behavior. That's because He's God!

Mother, listen to me. I know you would gladly die for the sake of your daughter. But would you die for the sake of the perverse man who raped and strangled her?

Father, listen well. I know you would give your life for your son. But what about the brutal man who kidnapped and killed him?

That's what God did! He didn't send Jesus to die for those who loved Him or sought Him or helped and served Him. He sent His Son to die for His murderers, for those who spat in His face and despised Him. That's the nature of God's love for us!

Governments often are quick to pay money to ransom a hostage or POW from the clutches of an enemy nation. But how much money do they spend seeking the release of hostile prisoners held captive in other countries?

Earlier I told you the story of Ah Ping, a teenage thug whose criminal life in Hong Kong was dramatically transformed when he heard of God's forgiving love. Ah Tong was also a member of the Triads. He was deeply addicted to heroin and financed his habit from the earnings of a fourteen-year-old prostitute whom he had once sold into a live sex show.[1]

In an effort to protect the life of a fellow gang member, Ah Tong was savagely beaten by several men with knives and water pipes. He miraculously survived.

A few years after the attack, Ah Tong wandered into Jackie Pullinger's youth club in the heart of the Walled City, desperate for help to kick his addiction to heroin.

Jackie seized the opportunity. "Ah Tong, what would you think about dying for someone in the other gang?" she asked.

"Tcha!" A wad of spit shot from his mouth as he looked bitterly at the missionary from England. "You must be joking! Your brother is one thing, but no one dies for his enemy!"

"Jesus did," said Jackie, and with that she proceeded to tell him of a love he never dreamed could exist. Ah Tong was initially stunned and shocked, but eventually saved by this unnatural love. He joined Ah Ping as a member of a new "gang," the church of Jesus Christ.[2]

What was it that attracted God to this world and its inhabitants? What was it that prompted Him to make the sacrifice of His Son for people like Ah Tong? People like you and me? Was it in response to some joint plea from mankind for help? Did God look down from heaven upon a sea of upraised hands pleading for deliverance? No! He saw only clenched fists of vile resistance. Was He moved by our good looks? Or did He see a divine "spark" flickering in our souls? No!

The only explanation why God loved us so as to give His Son is that He loved us so as to give His Son. No, that's not redundant. God loved us because God chose to love us because God is a God who loves.

I hope I've made this clear. It wasn't when or because you loved God that Jesus died for you but in spite of the fact that you and I were His bitterly entrenched enemies. If you understand that, you are ready for Paul to make his most poignant point.

THE LOGIC OF LOVE

> Since we have now been justified by his blood, how much
> more shall we be saved from God's wrath through him! For
> if, when we were God's enemies, we were reconciled to him
> through the death of his Son, how much more, having been
> reconciled, shall we be saved through his life!
>
> —ROMANS 5:9–11

If it is true and certain that you have been justified by faith in
Christ in the past, it is *much more* true and certain that you will
be delivered from God's wrath in the future.

Why is it much more certain? Because if Christ died for His
enemies you can bet your bottom dollar He'll save His *friends!* If
God did the greater thing in sending His Son to die for us while
we were His foes, how much easier will it be for Him to save us
now that we are His family!

If Christ *died* for you when you were an *alien,* how much more
shall He *live* for you now that you're an *ally!* If God loved us when
we were yet helplessly sinful, ungodly enemies, shall He not love
us now that by His grace we are justified and righteous in Christ?

Will the God who loved us and saved us when we were
orphans turn His back and desert us now that we are His children? Of course not! Paul's point is that if God has done the
greater thing for us He will most surely do the lesser.

If ever there were a time that God might not love you, it
would have been while you were an enemy and an alien, an outcast and an orphan, hostile and unholy. But even then He loved
you with an everlasting love and made the greatest imaginable
sacrifice in giving His own dear Son for your sinful soul. Now,
however, you are no longer an alien but a member of God's
household; no longer unreconciled but a child of the Father; no
longer at enmity but in love with the Lord of your life.

Later on in Romans, Paul makes the point once again:

> What, then, shall we say in response to this? If God is for
> us, who can be against us? He who did not spare his own

Son, but gave him up for us all—how will he not also, along
with him, graciously give us all things?

—ROMANS 8:31–32

If Paul had merely asked, "Will God give us all things?" we
might have wondered. We might have said to ourselves, *Well, you
know, I need so many things. How can I be certain God will provide
them?* But that isn't Paul's question. The God of whom Paul
speaks is the God "who did not spare his own Son, but gave him
up for us all!" The God who we ask if He will give us all things is
the God who has already given us His own Son!

Suppose one man possesses all the money in the world. He
freely and lovingly writes out a check to you in the amount of
five billion dollars. Elated, you ask him for a quarter so that you
might call your wife and break the good news. But he stingily
refuses. Absurd? Yes. But it is far more absurd to suggest that the
good and eternally gracious God who has given you His Son will
someday refuse to grant you what is needed to preserve your
soul. As J. W. Alexander put it:

> If a king were to give his feeble bride, who he had plucked
> with strong hand out of slavery, all his possessions, and a
> share of all his kingdom, surely she might rely on him for a
> piece of bread or a draught of water.[3]

I'm not saying you will always feel secure in God's love. God
wants you to, as I argue in the next chapter. Sometimes the tur-
bulence of your emotional life undermines your sense of security.
But God's love for you is an objective reality independent of your
subjective state of mind. God loves even those who doubt that
He loves them.

"But what about my sin? Doesn't God ever get so fed up with
my failures that He withdraws His love?" J. I. Packer answers
your question:

> When a Christian slips into sin, does that separate him from
> the love of God? In the fundamental sense, the answer is no,

because the Christian who is justified by faith has been accepted by God for all eternity into the divine family. So if he sins, he doesn't stop being a child of God; he just starts behaving like a bad child rather than a good one. His relationship with his father isn't destroyed, but it is spoiled until the wrong is acknowledged, forgiven, and set right. Bad children miss out on the good things that their parents are planning for them and need to be disciplined so that they may learn to be better children. So it is with God's children. But Christian prodigals, miserable as they make themselves, don't cease to be children of God or to be loved by Him.[4]

I know why you worry about the staying power of God's love. Perhaps you stood at an altar many years ago and listened as the person you loved with all your heart pledged his undying passion for you. Now he loves someone else.

Perhaps you recall the promise of your father that he would always be there to tuck you in at night and to watch you perform in the school play. Then one cold morning he was gone, and you haven't seen or heard from him in years.

It's tough to believe that God's love is any different from the love of others who in the end proved to be so unloving. We've been burned by the empty promises of other people and we fear that God is just like everyone else.

George Matheson was born in Glasgow, Scotland, on March 27, 1842. By the age of eighteen he was totally blind. Notwithstanding this disability, he went on to become a brilliant biblical scholar, pastor, and preacher.

Matheson was engaged to be married until his fiancé learned of his impending blindness. She left him. Needless to say, Matheson was devastated. The anguish inflicted by such fickle affection has the potential of souring our souls on God's love, too.

But not in George Matheson. Following this tragedy, he wrote one of the most touching hymns of the nineteenth century. The first verse says it all:

O Love that will not let me go,
I rest my weary soul in Thee;
I give Thee back the life I owe,
That in Thine ocean depths its flow
May richer, fuller be.[5]

WHEN THE HONEYMOON NEVER ENDS

ON A RECENT trip to Dallas I was anxious for our children to see the hotel where their mother and I had spent our honeymoon. When we arrived at the location we were crushed to discover that "progress" had turned our memory into a parking lot!

A lot of people would just as soon forget their honeymoon. The memory of what used to be is more than they can bear. The passion of those first few days of wedded bliss is gone. The intimacy they had hoped would last forever has faded. In a half-hearted effort to cloak their pain, they jokingly say, "Oh, well, the honeymoon is over!"

You may be inclined to think that way about your love affair with God, too. But for Him the honeymoon is never over! His love does not dwindle with time. Indeed, "As a bridegroom rejoices over his bride, so will your God rejoice over you" (Isa. 62:5).

I'm quite sure there are things about me now that Ann could never have foreseen, things that make it considerably more difficult for her to love me the way she did twenty-five years ago. As John Piper reminds us, "We can't sustain a honeymoon level of intensity and affection. We can't foresee the irritations that come with long-term familiarity. We can't stay as fit and handsome as we were then. We can't come up with enough new things to keep the relationship that fresh."[6]

But Isaiah 62:5 declares that God's love for you now is no less fervent than it was the first day you became His child. God is just as excited and enthusiastic about you today as He was yesterday. As Piper says, God "has no trouble sustaining a honeymoon level of intensity; He can foresee all the future quirks of our personality and has decided He will keep what's good for us and change what isn't; He will always be as handsome as He ever was, and will see to it that we get more and more beautiful forever; and He is infinitely creative to think of new things to do together so that there will be no boredom for the next trillion ages of millenniums."[7]

IN THE GRIP OF GOD'S LOVE

GOD DOESN'T WANT you to sit with a daisy in your hand, anxiously plucking petals, and saying, "He loves me; He loves me not. He loves me; He loves me not." Listen to how Paul drives home to our hearts the infallibility and immutability of God's love for us:

> Who shall separate us from the love of Christ? Shall trouble or hardship or persecution or famine or nakedness or danger or sword? As it is written: "For your sake we face death all day long; we are considered as sheep to be slaughtered." No, in all these things we are more than conquerors through him who loved us. For I am convinced that neither death nor life, neither angels nor demons, neither the present nor the future, nor any powers, neither height nor depth, nor anything else in all creation, will be able to separate us from the love of God that is in Christ Jesus our Lord.
>
> —ROMANS 8:35–39

Every time I read this I envision Paul sifting through the pages of some ancient dictionary or thesaurus, searching for yet another word, another synonym, to make his point clearer still. Leaving no theological stone unturned, Paul boldly insists that there is quite simply nothing—nowhere, no way, at no time—that can remove you from the firm but tender embrace of God's love.

"But I don't feel like a conqueror," comes the response. "I'm all too frequently conquered."

But look again, for it is "through him who loved us" that we conquer all enemies and overcome all obstacles. It isn't ultimately the strength of your grip on God that keeps you safe but God's grip on you.

Several years ago Ann and I took our daughter, Melanie, to the state fair of Texas. We had read a frightening report of what had happened to one child who was left to roam the fairgrounds unattended. Needless to say, I kept a firm grip on Melanie's tiny hand.

There were times when she struggled to break free. If given the chance she may well have wandered off into areas of potential danger. But my love for her infused an unbreakable strength into the grip I maintained on her hand. Her safety wasn't ultimately dependent on her determination to hold on to me. It was dependent on my resolve to hold on to her.

I love my children very much. Nothing short of death itself could have induced me to relax my grip. But my love for Melanie could well be called hatred when measured against the love of our heavenly Father for His kids.

Do you actually think God would ever let go of your hand and permit you to wander off into spiritual destruction? Do you actually think God's love for you, demonstrated in the death of Jesus while you were yet His enemy, could weaken now that you are His dearest and best friend?

No matter how hard you may struggle to break free, God's loving grip holds firm. No matter how alluring the amusements of this world may be, your Father will never permit you to be seduced so as to fall finally and fully away from Him. Take rest and joy in the reassuring words of Jesus:

> My sheep listen to my voice; I know them, and they follow me. I give them eternal life, and they shall never perish; no one can snatch them out of my hand. My Father, who has given them to me, is greater than all; no one can snatch them out of my Father's hand.
>
> —JOHN 10:27–29

ELIMINATING THE LAST LOOPHOLE

"BUT WHAT IF *I* decide to separate myself from the love of God? Could not *I* commit such sinful deeds that God would be left with no other choice but to cast me aside?" No. Again, no!

Paul knew you would ask that question. That's why he

included the phrase "nor anything else in all creation" (Romans 8:39). Let me ask you a silly question: "Are you a creature?" Well, of course, you are. There are only two classes of beings in existence: the Creator and the creatures. If you are not God, the Creator, then you are one of His creatures, a part of His creation. Therefore, this phrase includes you. Therefore, there is nothing that even *you* can do that would separate you from the love of God in Christ Jesus your Lord.

Paul has struggled to be as comprehensive as possible. Every conceivable chasm has been filled. All theological bases have been covered. Nothing that *is,* be it the smallest molecule or the mightiest man, whether demons or death, whether persecution or powers, can do anything to diminish or destroy God's love for you.

God has been singing to you for some time now. I hope you've paused to listen. Here's another one of His favorite tunes!

> The soul that on Jesus hath leaned for repose,
> I will not, I will not desert to its foes.
> That soul, though all hell should endeavor to shake,
> I'll never, no, never, no, never forsake![8]

Part Three:

Being Loved and Loving

12

Feeling Loved

I AM WRITING THIS chapter in mid-July in Missouri. It is *very* hot. In about two weeks my family and I will be making our way into the mountains of Colorado in search of cooler temperatures and a little relaxation. We intend to spend about a week in Estes Park, as we did two years ago.

Anyone who has been there will tell you there aren't many places in America more beautiful or more refreshing. On our first vacation there I was especially impressed by the roadside streams and rivers. It's hard to imagine anything anywhere surpassing them in terms of beauty and serenity. They were much the topic of conversation in our car as we drove through the mountains.

We talked about how clear and clean the water was and how cold it must be. We took pictures through the window of our car. We wondered aloud about the kind of fish one might catch and how dangerous the rapids would prove to someone in a canoe. Typical tourist talk.

But it wasn't good enough for my two daughters. They just

had to get out and play in the water. So we parked the car and prepared to get wet. It goes without saying that there is a world of difference between looking at those streams from inside a moving car and actually walking out into the middle of one. No matter how visually impressive they may be from the road, nothing compares with experiencing the water firsthand.

It's one thing to see it, but something else entirely to sit in those cold, refreshing streams. Watching is okay, but wading is better still. Taking pictures from afar is expected of people on vacation in Colorado. But bending down on one's hands and knees in the middle of a mountain stream and quenching your thirst is of a different order altogether.

So what does this have to do with God's love? Simply this. I don't want you to read this book and come away with the idea that God's love for you is simply something fascinating to think about, talk about, or merely look at as if it were a painting in an art gallery. I want you to *experience* it firsthand.

Certainly it's important for us to understand the meaning of divine love. We need to read about it in the Bible and meditate on it daily. But we mustn't settle for that. I don't want you to. More important still, *God* doesn't want you to.

God wants you to go beyond merely knowing that He loves you. He wants you to move past simply believing and affirming by faith that He loves you. He wants you to *taste* it! He wants you to get out of your car, take off your shoes and socks, jump in, and get wet! He wants you to *feel* the joy of being loved. He wants you to *receive* His love personally and powerfully in a way that is life changing. He wants you to wade in it, swim in it, and to be refreshed by drinking of it to your heart's delight and fill.

I'm overwhelmed to hear that God loves me. Sermons on God's love are uplifting and edifying. Writing a book about it has contributed immensely to my understanding and appreciation of the vast dimensions of God's commitment to my soul's ultimate and lasting welfare.

But that's not enough. It's not that I'm a demanding person by nature. I don't think my attitude is borne of sinful discontent. I honestly believe that the Holy Spirit is responsible for my craving to *feel* God's love. I yearn in the depths of my heart to experience in a passionate and powerful way the reality and presence of God's affection.

I know that I run the risk of being accused of anti-intellectualism or perhaps emotional fanaticism. But if you have paid any attention at all to what has preceded in this book you know how far from the truth that is. I have been careful to deal honestly with the text of Scripture. I have addressed your mind and challenged you to think reasonably and rationally about what God's love for us means and implies.

But there's more to it than that. We are more than our minds. There is more to being loved by the Creator of the universe than seeing it in the pages of the Bible or reading about it in the pages of this book. True love, genuine love is experienced love. Love that isn't felt may certainly be real, but it is just as certainly incomplete.

I want us to go beyond God's love as a mere spectacle. There is a dimension to being loved by God that transcends apprehending it intellectually. It is more than an objective fact, more than something "out there" to admire and observe. It is also a subjective experience, something "in here" to feel and enjoy.

My fear is that too many Christians experience God's love in the same way they do a great painting. If you have ever attended the exhibit of a famous art collection you know that extensive measures are employed to keep the viewing public at more than arm's length from the various works on display. Often, as with the Mona Lisa (in the Louvre in Paris, France), the painting is kept behind a glass enclosure. Security guards are positioned so that no one can get too close. Strategically placed signs warn of the consequences to be exacted from those who dare cross cordoned-off areas.

The result is that the viewing public is reduced to precisely that: viewing. They are mere spectators. I suppose in an art gallery that houses priceless masterpieces this is the only reasonable policy. But it won't do when it comes to God's love for His children. We cannot, we must not, allow ourselves to become spectators only. God's love is not to be viewed from afar but deeply and intimately embraced. Come close, touch, smell, feel, and enjoy the warmth of relationship with the author of this heavenly affection.

There are, however, two principal obstacles that must be overcome before some of you will accept what I'm saying. First, there is the fear people have of emotionalism. Most evangelical Christians are terrified of their feelings. They are suspicious of their emotional life and of anything of a subjective nature. I will need to address this at some length.

Second, I need to convince you from Scripture itself that *God wants you to feel loved.* There are several key texts that affirm the very thing I've been talking about, and we will look closely at them in the next chapter.

But let's first consider the nature and place of emotions in the Christian life. Do our feelings have anything to do with our faith? Or are they mortal enemies?

THE FEELINGS OF FAITH

DR. MARTYN LLOYD-JONES, long-time pastor of Westminster Chapel in London, England, once recalled an incident during the course of an evangelistic campaign in London. A prominent religious figure approached him and asked, "Have you been to the campaign?"

"No, not yet," replied Lloyd-Jones.

"It is marvelous," he said, "just marvelous! People are going forward by the hundreds, . . . and there is no emotion. It is simply marvelous!"

Lloyd-Jones was not impressed. His response to this man's endorsement of the campaign is instructive:

> What can one say about such an attitude? I content myself by asking a few questions. Can a man see himself as a damned sinner without emotion? Can a man listen to the thunderings of the Law and feel nothing? Or conversely, can a man really contemplate the love of God in Christ Jesus and feel no emotion? The whole position is utterly

ridiculous. I fear that many people today in their reaction against excesses and emotionalism put themselves into a position in which, in the end, they are virtually denying the Truth. The gospel of Jesus Christ takes up the whole man, and if what purports to be the gospel does not do so it is not the gospel. The gospel is meant to do that, and it does that. The whole man is involved because the gospel leads to regeneration; and so I say that this element of pathos and emotion, this element of being moved, should always be prominent in preaching.[1]

I agree with Lloyd-Jones. But I'm afraid we're in the minority. Whereas many may theoretically concur with his assessment, when it comes to their own religious experience, "emotion is regarded as something almost indecent."[2]

There is widespread belief that people who *feel passionately* do so as an excuse for not *thinking profoundly*. Evangelicals are frightened of their feelings, as if emotions were an alien element in their makeup, an intrusion, perhaps even a consequence of the Fall rather than a God-given aspect of the image of God in man.

For many Christians emotions are at best an inescapable and necessary evil. They are to be carefully monitored and ruthlessly suppressed. Anything that has the potential to arouse or stir up one's feelings is, at best, viewed with suspicion and, at worst, deemed demonic.

A few years ago I attended a church service with several friends, all of whom had been with me at a major theological conference. The church was known for many things, one of which was its commitment to the priority of corporate praise and worship. After about thirty minutes of what I thought was glorious and Christ-exalting worship, one man in our group turned to a close friend of mine and whispered, "Did you notice the *undulation* in the music?"

Undulation? What a strange word to describe a time of worship. But I knew why he used it. He was suspicious of anything that carried the potential to move him emotionally. He viewed such music as a threat to his determined resolve to keep control over his feelings. He was resistant to the emotional intensity and vulnerability that the praise songs might evoke in his own heart. What we might call the "spiritual atmosphere" of the service seemed inconsistent with his commitment to the primacy of the intellect (not to mention the image he wished to project to his academic colleagues present at the service).

This is just an example of what I sense is true of many, if not most, evangelical believers. You don't have to be a seminary or Bible-college professor to maintain this posture. I see it in Christians from every strata of church life. People are scared to death of their emotions. They've been warned and cautioned, most often from the pulpit, that any "feeling" beyond a controllable level of intensity is a dangerous threat to the "balanced" Christian life.

But why can't God be trusted with our emotions as much as He can with our minds? It seems as if evangelicals believe in God's sovereign control over everything *except* its effect on their feelings. What I'm contending for is that God can be trusted to direct and oversee our *experience* of His power as well as our *affirmation* of it.

Jack Hayford, pastor of Church On The Way in Van Nuys, California, has some helpful words of wisdom for us concerning this matter:

> It began to dawn on me that, given an environment where the Word of God was *foundational* and the Person of Christ the *focus*, the Holy Spirit could be trusted to do *both*—enlighten the intelligence and ignite the emotions. I soon discovered that to allow Him that much space necessitates more a surrender of my senseless fears than a surrender of sensible control. God is not asking any of us to abandon reason or succumb to some euphoric feeling. He is, however, calling us to trust Him—enough to give *Him* control.[3]

So what becomes of "feeling" loved by God? Ought we to abandon any hope of such an experience? Is it "imbalanced" and "extreme" even to think about, much less seek, the joy and ecstasy of God's affection for us? This is a difficult issue that demands our careful attention.

WHAT DOES EMOTION MEAN?

AN EMOTION IS a sensation of the mind that often but not always has an impact on the body. An emotion or affection is more than a mere thought or idea or intellectual notion in our heads. It is a lively and vigorous activity of the mind in which we are, in varying degrees, either delighted or displeased with something.

Such emotions as love, joy, desire, gratitude, hate, sorrow, grief, revulsion, and anger normally, but not always, have a bodily impact. God "feels" deeply and passionately but has no physical body. The quadriplegic, who has a body but no physical sensations in those areas that are paralyzed, still experiences deep emotions. And the "dead in Christ," those in heaven with the Lord in a *disembodied* state, certainly experience joy and delight. (See Philippians 1:21–26.)

Where people go astray is in assigning to their emotional life an authority that God never intended. This is true primarily in two areas.

First of all, our emotions are not an infallible guide for establishing what is true or false. Doctrine is not derived from our feelings or our passions. The Bible and the Bible alone is the ultimate standard by which we can discover inerrant truth.

Certainly our experience can *confirm* truth and even shed additional light on its meaning. Occasionally we never really appreciate the implications of some theological principle until we feel its impact in the rigors of daily living. But our experience in and of itself does *not create* truth.

There have been times when my experience has awakened me to some biblical truth that, though I knew it to *be* truth, was never a vital part of my understanding of what it means to live a Christian life. I think immediately of James 5:13–18 and the so-called "prayer of faith."

I exegeted the text, defined its terms, but never fully understood its power until God enabled me to pray just such a prayer on that occasion when He healed an infant boy in our church of a serious liver disease.

But again, let us remember that feelings alone are not decisive in determining doctrinal verities. Otherwise, most would conclude that the existence of hell was a myth. It is difficult to "feel good" about the idea of eternal torment! But we know hell is real because the Bible says so.

What I see happening with many Christians is the tendency to employ their emotions for purposes that God intended the Bible to achieve. Be very careful, therefore, lest you rely on how you feel to decide what is true and what is false.[4]

Second, our emotions are not an infallible standard for determining God's attitude toward us. Simply because you are feeling depressed does not necessarily mean God is angry with you. Feelings of loneliness and fear and doubt and the like are not always signs of God's displeasure.

Nor is it always the case that feeling good and glad is the fruit of God's favor. Sin feels good. If sin were incapable of producing pleasure, we wouldn't commit it! So, again, don't use your emotions to tell you what the Bible was designed to say.

WHAT IS THE PLACE FOR OUR PASSIONS?

MOST INSIST THAT our emotions and passions should be given, at best, a subordinate role in the Christian life. I disagree. Following the lead of the seventeenth-century Puritan pastor and theologian Jonathan Edwards, I want to suggest that true religion, true Christianity, consists of the enjoyment of *sanctified emotions*. Edwards called them *holy affections*.

Look carefully at what the apostle Peter says in his first epistle. After describing our salvation in Christ and the hope of entering into the full inheritance of what God has promised, Peter says:

> In this you greatly rejoice, though now for a little while you
> may have had to suffer grief in all kinds of trials. These have
> come so that your faith—of greater worth than gold, which

perishes even though refined by fire—may be proved genuine and may result in praise, glory and honor when Jesus Christ is revealed. Though you have not seen him, you love him; and even though you do not see him now, you believe in him and are filled with an inexpressible and glorious joy, for you are receiving the goal of your faith, the salvation of your souls.

—1 PETER 1:6–9

If you look closely at what Peter is saying you will see that he is describing *love* for Christ and *joy* in Christ, two "sanctified emotions," as the essence of being a Christian.

Peter is writing to believers who are enduring persecution and oppression. (See 1 Peter 2:20–21; 3:17; 4:12–18.) He first encourages them with the reminder that such trials are temporary ("for a little while," v. 6). More important still is that their afflictions serve to purify their faith. (See Psalm 119:67, 71, 75.) What he tells them, in effect, is that God never wastes pain.

He does this by drawing an analogy between what suffering does to a Christian and what fire does to gold. Fire burns away the dross and alloy from gold, leaving it pure and solid. In similar fashion, the flames of trial and testing and affliction burn away the dross from our faith. Hypocrisy, pride, and other spurious elements are consumed, leaving behind the solid element of raw dependency on Christ alone. (See Psalm 66:10; Isaiah 48:10; Malachi 3:3.)

So when Peter comes to verse eight he is describing for us Christian life and faith in its purest form (this side of heaven). This verse is the portrait of a child of God who has been rid of as much sinful dross as is possible short of glorification.

Here is faith as it has never been seen before, with the rough edges pared off. This is the Christian with no additives or preservatives—grade *A* faith, the genuine item, the real McCoy!

Another way of describing it is to envision the Christian as a block of granite or marble that comes under assault from a hammer and chisel (suffering in its many forms). What we find in verse eight is what's left after the sculptor finishes his work.

Think of an athlete who has done nothing for weeks. He is overweight. His muscles have atrophied. He is heavy-legged; his lung capacity has greatly diminished. But rigorous training results in a finely-honed body, ready for competition. What training does for the athlete's body suffering does for the Christian's soul.

Therefore that which characterizes Christian faith and life in its purest form, as free from error and evil and impurity as possible, is wholehearted *love* for Christ and an inexpressibly glorious *joy* in Christ. That's just another way of saying that the quintessence of Christianity is the enjoyment of sanctified emotions!

I'm not saying that our joy is in joy, but in *God*. I'm not suggesting we put our joy above God's glory but rather *in* God's glory. "Our quest," says John Piper, "is not merely joy. It is joy in God. And there is no way for a creature to consciously manifest the infinite worth and beauty of God without delighting in Him."[5]

So much of what passes for Christianity today is little more than pious morbidity. Evangelicals seem to be afraid of enjoying God. They are paralyzed by the fear of emotionalism. But let's think about this for a moment.

THE ERROR OF EMOTIONALISM

EMOTIONALISM IS THE artificial manipulation of feeling for the feeling's sake. I saw an example of this several years ago during a religious celebration in Tehran, Iran. Some Shiite Muslims were stirring themselves into an emotional and mindless frenzy to prepare for an act of self-mutilation. When they had reached a point where they were evidently oblivious to pain, they began to slit their scalps with razors and beat themselves on the head with the flat side of a sword, all in honor of a dead hero.

But the only emotions and passions that please God are those that are rooted in biblical truth. They must arise from a thinking, perceptive understanding of who God is and be the fruit of a personal encounter with Him. Religious affections that do not come from reflective meditation on God are neither helpful nor holy.

For emotional heat to be holy it must be the product of

theological light. Spiritual feelings must arise out of our perception of spiritual facts. High and noble thoughts about God are inseparably linked to deep and pleasurable feelings for Him. Holy affections are the consummate consequence of an enlightened mind.

THE ENJOYMENT OF EMOTIONS

WHAT WE MUST remember is that to fill the mind is to thrill the soul! God built you with the capacity to feel and experience spiritual ecstasy so that He might be glorified in your enjoyment of Him! Emotions are to be enjoyed. Feelings are for fun.

Don't take my word for it. Listen to what God commends and commands relative to your emotional life:

> You have made known to me the path of life; you will fill me with joy in your presence, with eternal pleasures at your right hand.
>
> —PSALM 16:11

> Delight yourself in the LORD and he will give you the desires of your heart.
>
> —PSALM 37:4

> They feast on the abundance of your house; you give them drink from your river of delights.
>
> —PSALM 36:8

Elsewhere the psalmist speaks about a passionate yearning for God that can only be compared to the relentless search for water by a thirsty deer (Ps. 42:1–2; 63:1). We are to "taste and see that the LORD is good" (Ps. 34:8) and to find in Him "exceeding joy" (Ps. 43:4, NAS).

After Jesus revealed His identity to the two disciples on the Emmaus road they exclaimed, "Were not our hearts burning within us while he talked with us on the road and opened the Scriptures to us?" (Luke 24:32). Their minds were enlightened to understand and they *felt* the effects of it in their whole being. This is what I call a case of "spiritual heartburn!" But whatever you do, don't take a Tums! Enjoy the heat!

What did they feel? Perhaps they experienced a rapid heartbeat, chills down their spine, maybe even bodily weakness that made it difficult to stand erect. Their breathing may have quickened as they began to feel lightheaded. Perhaps they trembled and wept and rejoiced.

Does your heart "burn" within when you think of God singing in love over you? It should. It's okay. God wants it to. Deep down inside I suspect you want it to also. God longs for you to feel deep and lasting satisfaction in Him. That is the principal way He is glorified in you. So enjoy Him. Receive His love for you and revel in it. Let His affection for your soul lift you to unknown heights of spiritual ecstasy. Honor Him by being happy in Him.

Let me close by returning to the story of our trip to Colorado with which I began and simply say: Get out of the car! Get on your knees and drink the cool, refreshing waters of God's love! It tastes so good! It quenches the thirsty soul and renews the sagging spirit! And best of all, it glorifies God.

13

The Joy of Receiving God's Love

SOMEONE ONCE referred to a friend of mine as a person who "does not receive well." At first it struck me as an odd way of describing anyone, but on further reflection I had to agree. The lady he had in mind is a giver. She loves to give and does so generously. She gives at great cost to herself, both physically and financially. But he was right. She doesn't "receive" well.

I'm not sure why she has difficulty in letting others do for her what she so graciously does for them. Perhaps she feels unworthy or undeserving of their gifts. I've watched her when people have offered their help, and it's obvious she's uncomfortable and ill at ease with it all. I suspect there are a lot just like her.

I *know* there are when it comes to receiving God's love. Most Christians rejoice in telling others that God loves them. But it's hard for them to sit still and relax in the love that God has for *them* personally.

This was especially evident to me one Saturday night during the course of a praise service at church. On this particular evening we had sung several songs that affirmed our love for the Father. It seemed natural and proper to do so. But toward the close of the service we sang a new song in which we were to receive the Father's love for us. It was a powerfully moving occasion that I will not soon forget. The chorus was short and simple. Here are the lyrics:

> O Lord, Your tenderness,
> Melting all my bitterness,
> O Lord, I receive Your love.
> O Lord, Your loveliness,
> Changing my unworthiness,
> O Lord, I receive Your love.
> O Lord, I receive Your love,
> O Lord, I receive Your love.[1]

As we sang softly, the Holy Spirit did what no human could hope to achieve. He enthroned Himself on our praise and moved powerfully in the hearts of all who were present. Tears flowed freely and all resistance melted as each of us, some for the first time, received the Father's love. For that one moment we stopped giving. God was the only giver. We stood, sat, and knelt in stunned ecstasy as the Father embraced His children. It was an unspeakably glorious and life-changing moment.

No one present that night was untouched. It was emotionally intense and inescapably palpable. Most important of all, God was honored. Our souls found indescribable satisfaction in His affection for us, and therein the children magnified the Father's all-sufficiency.

That's what these two chapters on feeling loved are all about. I'm convinced the Bible tells us that God wants us to feel His love, and that He has taken all the necessary steps to see that we do. In chapter twelve I argued that it's not only okay to emotionally enjoy God's love—it's essential.

In this chapter I want to explore with you several texts of Scripture that affirm this truth as well as suggest what to do if God's love feels distant, if not dead.

FLOODED WITH THE FATHER'S LOVE

OUR FIRST TEXT is perhaps the most important one of all. It is found in Romans 5:5.

> And hope does not disappoint us, because God has poured out his love into our hearts by the Holy Spirit, whom he has given us.

How do we know that our hope in Christ won't fall apart? How do we know it all won't fizzle out in the end or be consumed by the fires of God's wrath on the final day? We know, says Paul, by virtue of the action God has taken to assure us of His eternal and unchanging love. This love He poured out into our hearts through the Holy Spirit.

Other English translations are unclear whether it is God's love for us or our love for God that Paul has in mind. But the NIV is certainly correct, and for two reasons.

First, "the love of God" is designed to be a proof of the security of our hope. How can *our* loving God do that? Our love for God is fitful and often faint. If my hope is built on how well I love God, there will be times when I will be quite hopeless.

Second, verses six through eleven are an obvious expansion of the nature of this love in verse five. There, clearly it is God's love for us as demonstrated by the gracious gift of His Son to die in our stead.

Now that we've settled the fact that it is God's love for us, observe how Paul describes what God has done to make it possible for us to experience it "up close and personal."

He tells us that God "poured out" His love "into our hearts." The verb *poured out* is used elsewhere of the spilling of wine (Luke 5:37), the shedding of Christ's blood (Matt. 26:28), and of the pouring out of the Holy Spirit at Pentecost (Acts 10:45). More graphic still is its use in Acts 1:18 of the fate of Judas: "With the reward he got for his wickedness, Judas bought a field; there he fell headlong, his body burst open and all his intestines *spilled out*" (emphasis added).

Paul is emphasizing the unstinting lavishness with which God has flooded our hearts with a sense of His love for us.

"The hearts of believers," writes John Murray, "are regarded as being suffused with the love of God; it controls and captivates their hearts."[2]

"Like an overflowing stream in a thirsty land," says Gifford, "so is the rich flood of divine love poured out and shed abroad in the heart."[3]

This is an exuberant communication of God's love.

The love of God, writes Charles Hodge, "does not descend upon us as dew drops, but as a stream which spreads itself abroad through the whole soul, filling it with the consciousness of His presence and favour."[4]

God wants *your* heart to be inundated by wave after wave of His fatherly affection, so effusively poured out that you feel compelled to request that He pull back lest you drown in His passion!

Paul is not talking "of faint and fitful impressions," says Packer, "but of deep and overwhelming ones."[5]

I suspect that the famous evangelist Dwight L. Moody (1837–1899) knew precisely what Paul meant. Moody was always reluctant to speak of what occurred, but he conceded to give the following brief account:

> One day, in the city of New York—oh, what a day!—I can't describe it, I seldom refer to it; it is almost too sacred an experience to name . . . I can only say that God revealed Himself to me, and I had such an experience of His love that I had to ask Him to stay His hand. I went to preaching again. The sermons were not different; I did not present any new truths, and yet hundreds were converted. I would not now be placed back where I was before that blessed experience if you should give me all the world—it would be small dust in the balance.[6]

It's also important to note that Paul uses the perfect tense of the verb. This implies, Packer explains:

A settled state consequent upon a completed action. The thought is that knowledge of the love of God, having flooded our hearts, *fills them now,* just as a valley once flooded remains full of water. Paul assumes that all his readers, like himself, will be living in the enjoyment of a strong and abiding sense of God's love for them.[7]

In other words, God's love doesn't leak! Unlike the waters of Noah that receded after a time, God's love remains perpetually at flood stage in our souls!

The Holy Spirit works to evoke and stimulate in your heart the overwhelming conviction that God loves you. The amplitude and immensity of God's devotion is not abstract and generic, but concrete and personal . . . not for everyone in general but for *you* in particular.

I've always found it difficult to describe more precisely what Paul is saying here. Perhaps this is because he's not talking about knowledge that we gain by inference from a body of evidence. Neither deduction nor induction can account for what he has in mind. Empirical observation doesn't yield the assurance of being God's beloved.

The *objective* proof of God's love is the sacrificial gift of His Son (Rom. 5:6–8). Like many of you I grew up in a church singing, "Jesus loves me; this I know, for the Bible tells me so." I still rejoice in that truth. But the phenomenon portrayed in Romans 5:5 is altogether *subjective* in nature. This is an assurance of being God's beloved that is fundamentally *intuitive*. One knows it to be true because through the internal work of the Spirit one knows it to be true!

LOVED LIKE JESUS

DID YOU KNOW that God's love has a goal? God does not love us aimlessly. The apostle John speaks of God's love being perfected or coming to full expression in us. Look at what he says:

By this, love is perfected with us, that we may have

confidence in the day of judgment; because as He [Jesus] is, so also are we in this world.

—1 JOHN 4:17, NAS

I believe that John is saying much the same that Paul said in Romans 5:5. The Father's love for His children reaches its intended goal when it produces in them a feeling of security so powerful that they lose all fear of judgment. When our sense of being loved by God becomes so *internally intense* that we can only smile at the prospect of judgment day, His passion has fulfilled its purpose!

Someone might think it presumptuous to have lost all fear of judgment. But John clearly says that our confidence is based on the *fact* that the believer is "as He [Jesus] is."

What could that possibly mean? In what sense is the Christian "as Jesus is" in the world?

John may mean that we are righteous as Jesus is righteous. By faith in Him we are justified, declared righteous in the sight of God, and therefore we look forward to judgment day confident that there is now no condemnation for those who are in Christ Jesus (Rom. 8:1). That's possible, but I think the answer lies elsewhere.

Look again at 1 John 4:17. John is saying that our confidence is linked with God's love for us, and that in some sense we are as Jesus is. These two pieces of the puzzle are put together in John 17:23 where Jesus affirms that the Father loves the disciples "even as you [the Father] have loved me [Jesus]."

This is astounding! Jesus is saying that the Father loves us *just like* or *even as* He loves Jesus! Think for a moment of the magnitude of affection God the Father has for God the Son. That's how much God loves you!

Therefore when John says that our confidence is based on the fact that *we* are as *Jesus* is, he means *we are loved by the Father as Jesus is loved by the Father!*

No wonder all fear is cast out (1 John 4:18).

There is no need to fear Him who you know feels only love for you.

THE CONFIDENT CRY OF A CHILD

I HAVE ALREADY spoken of God's adopting love and the joy of knowing we are His children. But look again at what the apostle says of this in Romans 8:15–16.

> For you did not receive a spirit that makes you a slave again to fear, but you received the Spirit of sonship. And by him we cry, "Abba, Father." The Spirit himself testifies with our spirit that we are God's children.

I doubt that anything can rival the delight that erupts in our hearts when we finally realize we are God's children. Here Paul talks about knowing, deep down inside, that God is our Father. It isn't something we crank up or work out or pull down. It is the work of the Holy Spirit in our spirit.

God tells us that whoever believes in Christ Jesus is saved. We believe. And then, as if to ratify, strengthen, and intensify that certainty the Holy Spirit says to our spirit, "Yes! Yes! You are indeed God's child. He is indeed your Father!" It isn't via the text of Scripture that He does this, but directly and subjectively, in and to and on and through our hearts.

This unshakeable assurance that we are sons and daughters of God is not a conclusion we draw from the fact that we cry "Abba! Father!" Rather, our childlike cry of "Abba!" is the fruit of that conviction. A confident cry indeed.

KNOWING THE UNKNOWABLE

LET'S EAVESDROP ON the apostle Paul as he prays for you and me in Ephesians 3:16–19.

> I pray that out of his glorious riches he may strengthen you with power through his Spirit in your inner being, so that Christ may dwell in your hearts through faith. And I pray that you, being rooted and established in love, may have power, together with all the saints, to grasp how wide and

long and high and deep is the love of Christ, and to know
this love that surpasses knowledge—that you may be filled
to the measure of all the fullness of God.

Paul prays for several things here, all of which pertain to our
sensible experience of the person of Christ. He prays that we
might be internally strengthened by the Spirit so that Christ
might dwell in our hearts. But how can that be if we have *already*
received Christ into our hearts when we were born again?

The only viable explanation is that Paul is referring to an
experiential enlargement of what is already theologically true. He
wants us to be strengthened by the Spirit so that Jesus might
exert a progressively greater and more intense personal influence
in our souls.

The result of this expansion of the divine power and presence in
our hearts is the ability to "grasp how wide and long and high and
deep" Christ's love for us really is. Again, this is Paul's way of
saying that God intends for us to feel and experience and be emotionally moved by the passionate affection He has for us, His
children. D. A. Carson, in my view, is right on target when he says:

> This cannot be merely an intellectual exercise. Paul is not
> asking that his readers might become more able to articu-
> late the greatness of God's love in Christ Jesus or to grasp
> with the intellect alone how significant God's love is in the
> plan of redemption. He is asking God that they might have
> the power to grasp the dimensions of that love in their
> experience. Doubtless that includes intellectual reflection,
> but it cannot be reduced to that alone.[8]

But how are we to compute such love? What are its dimensions? Does it come in meters or miles? Do we measure it in
yards or pounds? Does Paul intend for you to think in terms of
mathematical proportions, as if to suggest that God loves you
one hundred times more than He loves the angels or fifty times
less than He loves a purportedly more godly Christian?

Quite to the contrary, says Paul. There is a width and length and height and depth to Christ's love for you that goes beyond human measurement. The immensity and magnitude of that love in incalculable. Its dimensions defy containment. It is beyond knowing. Yet Paul prays that we might *know* it! This deliberate oxymoron serves to deepen what is already too deep to fathom.

Andrew Lincoln summed it up best by saying, "It is simply that the supreme object of Christian knowledge, Christ's love, is so profound that its depths will never be sounded and so vast that its extent will never be encompassed by the human mind."[9]

LIVING IN THE LOVE OF GOD

ON THE NIGHT Jesus was betrayed, He spoke these words of comfort to His disciples:

> As the Father has loved me, so have I loved you. Now remain in my love. If you obey my commands, you will remain in my love, just as I have obeyed my Father's commands and remain in his love. I have told you this so that my joy may be in you and that your joy may be complete.
>
> —JOHN 15:9–11

What does Jesus mean when He tells us to "remain" or "abide" in His love? He can't mean that we are to do things to persuade Him to love us. We do not prompt God's love. Love is all of grace, as we have seen time and again. It flows from God's sovereign and free choice. Nor can He mean that we are to work so that God's love won't diminish or disappear. His love is eternal.

It would seem, then, that He is telling us to live in His love, that is, to enjoy it, to bask in its soothing and reassuring warmth. The key to unlock the door to this delight of the soul is obedience. This isn't to suggest that our works woo God or in some sense win His love.

God's love is like the light of the sun. It shines constantly and incessantly. On occasion it is obscured from view, like the clouds that make for an overcast day. We are to be especially diligent not to hide in the shade of disobedience and disbelief. Doing what Christ has commanded enables us to enjoy and to feel the love that never leaves.

Another reason for believing that Jesus has in view our *experience* of divine love is the reference to "joy" in verse 11. The joy of Jesus is His delight in being loved by His Father. He too remains in that love (John 15:10). Our joy, therefore, is our delight in being loved by both Father and Son. (See John 14:23.) *Jesus wants us to enjoy the joy of being enjoyed by God!* What joy!

This is what I think Jude is describing in verse 21 of his short epistle. There he commands us to "keep" ourselves "in God's love." He can't mean we are to make ourselves loveable. As we've already seen in Roman 5:6–8, it was while we were altogether unloveable that He loved us with an everlasting and unconditional love.

Once again, we must be reminded that God's love for us in Christ is an objective fact that nothing in all of creation can alter (Rom. 8:35–39). This leaves us with only one alternative. Jude, like Jesus, must be referring to the subjective apprehension of God's love. Do what you must, says Jude, to avail yourself of the unparalleled joy of receiving the love of God.

That this experience is ultimately a work of God the Father, through the Holy Spirit, is confirmed by Paul's prayer in 2 Thessalonians 3:5:

> May *the Lord* direct your hearts into God's love and Christ's perseverance.
>
> —EMPHASIS ADDED

In the final analysis, if we are to "feel" loved of the Father it is the Father Himself who must (and will) act to remove every obstacle and clear away every encumbrance to that inexpressible experience. *I* can't do it. Reading this book can't do it. God must do it.

The obstacles to this are very real indeed. Preeminent among them are those concocted by Satan himself. Receiving God's love is difficult when the enemy has filled your mind with lies about how much He hates you. Satan's greatest ploy is to deceive the

Christian into thinking that he or she is a pathetic embarrassment to the Father, little more than useless, dead weight on the body of Christ.

Satan will do everything within his diabolical power to sow the seeds of helplessness and hopelessness in your heart. He will remind you incessantly of past failures, insisting that God cannot love anyone who has so frequently fouled things up. He will make hay with what I call "satanic toos"—"You're *too* ugly for God to love, *too* dumb, *too* fat, *too* poor, *too* weak, *too* untalented, and worst of all, even if you overcome these deficiencies, you're *too* late!"

Paul's prayer is that God would Himself act to obliterate all such obstacles to the enjoyment of being loved. Surely, then, we must begin to pray for ourselves and for one another even as Paul prayed for the Thessalonians.

A FINAL WORD ON "HOW TO"

I'VE DEVOTED TWO chapters to the importance of feeling God's love. Still, though, there are many who even now are saying to themselves, "But what do I do when I don't feel loved?" Here are some suggestions.

First: *Remind and refresh yourself of the* fact *of God's undying love,* notwithstanding your inability to *feel* it. Go back and read again the first eleven chapters of this book. The seed of feeling is always in faith. So begin by reaffirming what you know is true. Even though it may seem hypocritical and empty, do it. Defy what you feel and cling in faith to Zephaniah 3:17.

As you take this first step, let me remind you of something absolutely crucial. As I've said before, God's love for you does not depend on your ability to believe it or feel it. Don't make the mistake of thinking that His love hangs suspended on the thin thread of your devotion to Him. God's love for you is not a reflex response to your love for Him.

Perhaps the greatest obstacle to enjoying God's love is our mistaken belief that we have to be a delight to ourselves before we can be a delight to God. We know ourselves all too painfully well. We look at our faults and failures and say, "If *I* were God *I* wouldn't love me!" We think that only after we have done those things that enable us to enjoy ourselves can God enjoy us. But God does not see us as we see ourselves. He sees us in His Son. Never let your feelings for yourself be the barometer of God's ability to love.

Second: *Obey.* Jesus said in John 15 that the key to enjoying the joy of being enjoyed by God is obedience. It may well be that sin has numbed your soul and deadened your spiritual senses. So examine yourself, confess your sins, and again claim by faith that your Father has forgiven them (1 John 1:9).

Third: *Pray.* Come before the Lord and ask Him to restore unto you the joy of your salvation. Plead with Him for a fresh outpouring and infilling of His Spirit that you might once again know the unknowable dimensions of His love for you.

Fourth: *Worship your way into the experience of His love.* Take up the name of God on your lips and ascribe to Him the glory due His name. God has promised to enthrone Himself in our praise and to release His irresistible power upon the sound of our songs.

Sometimes we sink so low that we must worship *to* joy rather than *from* joy. It is often "out of the depths" that we praise God, and not always from "atop the heights." So tell of His worth, confident that when God hears you sing of His love He will, eventually, enable you to feel it as well.

Fifth: *Wait.* The other four steps come easily compared with the fifth. But we must wait. We must patiently persevere, knowing that God will renew and reinvigorate and revive and rekindle the flame that once burned bright. So wait. And meditate on the words of Jeremiah:

> I remember my affliction and my wandering, the bitterness and the gall. I well remember them, and my soul is downcast within me. Yet this I call to mind and therefore I have hope: Because of the LORD'S great love we are not consumed, for his compassions never fail. They are new every morning; great is your faithfulness. I say to myself, "The LORD is my portion; therefore I will wait for him."
> —LAMENTATIONS 3:19–24

Addendum

Felt Love in the Life
of Sarah Edwards

I SENSE A REAL urgency to put flesh and blood and bones on these past two chapters. What we need is not merely truth but *incarnate* truth. That is, we need to see what these truths look like when they adorn the soul of a human being just like you and me.

I have someone particular in mind. Her name was Sarah Edwards, wife of Puritan pastor and theologian, Jonathan Edwards. Sarah's experience of God's love came in the wake of the revival known as the First Great Awakening that broke out in New England in the late 1730s and early 1740s.

Jonathan was so impressed and in awe of what God had done in his wife that he prevailed upon her to write it down. Sarah's testimony is too lengthy to reproduce here in its entirety, so I have excerpted only those sections that pertain to what I have been calling "felt love." I encourage you, though, to take time to read the full narrative of her experience.[1] It is rich and rewarding.

Please do not think that I am setting forth Sarah Edwards as the norm for all Christians of every age. Having said that, I must admit I envy her. My heart's desire is to be "filled to the measure of all the fullness of God" as she was (Eph. 3:19). But we must leave it to God to deal with each of us as individuals.

Opinions vary of Sarah and her experience of God's love. Some, such as I, read it and say, "I want that!" Others are more reluctant: "Come on, Sarah, get hold of yourself!" My personal convictions are that it was truly God who "got hold" of Sarah Edwards. But you be the judge.

Sarah's experience began with a renewed sense of what she called "the riches of full assurance" of salvation. It was evoked by a meditation on Romans 8:34. The day was January 20, 1742.

> When I was alone, the words came to my mind with far greater power and sweetness; upon which I took the Bible, and read the words to the end of the chapter, when they were impressed on my heart with vastly greater power and sweetness still. They appeared to me with undoubted certainty as the words of God, and as words which God did pronounce concerning me. I had no more doubt of it, than I had of my being. I seemed as it were to hear the great God proclaiming thus to the world concerning me: "Who shall lay any thing to thy charge," and had it strongly impressed on me, how impossible it was for any thing in heaven or earth, in this world or the future, ever to separate me from the love of God which was in Christ Jesus. I cannot find language to express, how certain this appeared—the everlasting mountains and hills were but shadows to it. My safety, and happiness, and eternal enjoyment of God's immutable love, seemed as durable and unchangeable as God Himself. Melted and overcome by the sweetness of this assurance, I fell into a great flow of tears, and could not forebear weeping aloud. It appeared certain to me that God was my Father, and Christ my Lord and Savior, that He was mine and I His.

On one occasion the words to a hymn awakened Sarah to the reality of God's love for her.

And while I was uttering the words, my mind was so deeply impressed with the love of Christ, and a sense of His immediate presence, that I could with difficulty refrain from rising from my seat and leaping for joy. I continued to enjoy this intense, and lively, and refreshing sense of divine things, accompanied with strong emotions, for nearly an hour; after which, I experienced a delightful calm, and peace and rest in God, until I retired for the night; and during the night, both waking and sleeping, I had joyful views of divine things, and a complacent rest of soul in God. I awoke in the morning of Thursday, January 28th in the same happy frame of mind, and engaged in the duties of my family with a sweet consciousness that God was present with me, and with earnest longings of soul for the continuance and increase of the blessed fruits of the Holy Spirit in the town.

Sarah then proceeds to describe what occurred that night, "the sweetest night I ever had in my life." Her language is a bit unusual and the imagery is startling, but such is the struggle one faces in trying to articulate "joy inexpressible and full of glory" (1 Pet. 1:8, NAS).

I never before, for so long a time together, enjoyed so much of the light, and rest, and sweetness of heaven in my soul, but without the least agitation of body during the whole time. The great part of the night I lay awake, sometimes asleep, and sometimes between sleeping and waking. But all night I continued in a constant, clear and lively sense of the heavenly sweetness of Christ's excellent and transcendent love, of His nearness to me, and of my dearness to Him; with an inexpressibly sweet calmness of soul in an entire rest in Him. I seemed to myself to perceive a glow of divine love come down from the heart of Christ in heaven, into my heart, in a constant stream, like a stream or pencil of sweet light. At the same time, my heart and soul all flowed out in love to Christ; so that there seemed to be a constant flowing and reflowing of heavenly and divine love, from Christ's heart to mine; and I appeared to myself to float or swim, in these bright, sweet beams of the love of Christ, like the motes swimming in the beams of the sun, or the streams of His light which come in at the window. My soul remained in a kind of heavenly elysium. So far as I am capable of making a comparison, I think that what I felt each minute, during the continuance of the whole time, was worth more than all the outward comfort and pleasure, which I had enjoyed in my whole life put together. It was a pure delight, which fed and satisfied the soul. It was pleasure, without the least sting, or any interruption. It was a sweetness, which my soul was lost in. It seemed to be all that my feeble frame could sustain, of that fulness of joy, which is felt by those who behold the face of Christ, and share His love in the heavenly world. There was but little difference, whether I was asleep or awake, so deep was the impression made on my soul; but if there was any difference, the sweetness was greatest and must uninterrupted while I was asleep.

As I said, these are but a few selections from a much larger word of testimony. But it is enough to illustrate and express what I have meant by the terminology, "felt love."

If you still regard her experience as excessive and imbalanced, at least listen to what her husband, Jonathan, said of it. He was, according to many, the greatest theological mind since the apostle Paul. He was not given to fanaticism or delusion. Consider his assessment carefully. As for me, I agree.

Now if such things [as Sarah experienced] are enthusiasm [Edwards' word for "emotionalism"], and the offspring of a distempered brain, let my brain be possessed evermore of that happy distemper! If this be distraction, I pray God that the world of mankind may all be seized with this benign, meek, beneficent, beatific, glorious distraction!

14

The Singing Saint

G OD'S LOVE NEVER leaves us where we are. It always leads us to places we've never been. It never lies dormant in the soul. It penetrates deeply and impregnates its host with an irresistible urge to love others with the love with which it has been loved.

God's love transforms sinners into saints and lovers of self into selfless lovers. It turns takers inside out and makes them glad givers. People who used to ask, "What's in it for me?" now say, "What's in it for me is the unparalleled joy that comes from being more concerned about what's in it for them!"

All this is to say that God's love is never merely vertical. God's love is less like a lightning bolt that strikes from heaven and more like the rain that first falls vertically and then floods horizontally until all are wet.

This is what the apostle John had in mind when he said that "no one has ever seen God; but if we love one another, God lives in us and his love is made complete in us" (1 John 4:12). Other texts also insist that God has never been seen. (See 1 Timothy 1:17;

6:16; Exodus 33:20.) How, then, can God be known? In John 1:18 the answer is given: "No one has ever seen God, but God the One and Only, who is at the Father's side, has made him known."

The fact that God can't be seen except in the face of Jesus is all well and good. It makes for fascinating theological conversation. But what does it have to do with you and me loving other people?

Evidently what the apostle is saying is that the unseen God, revealed once in His Son, "is now revealed in His people if and when they love one another. God's love is seen in their love because their love is His love imparted to them by His Spirit."[1]

The point seems to be that although God cannot be seen in Himself, He *can* be seen in those in whom He abides when they love others with that very love wherewith they were loved! Technically speaking, God is invisible. But if you want to know what He's like, look at Christian lovers. In them, and particularly in their love, the fullness of God's affection takes on a bodily form.

God's love has showered us with salvation. We revel in the new life He has graciously granted. But life alone is not the ultimate aim of God's grace. Love is. God's love is made complete in us when we obey His Word to love others as He has loved us (1 John 2:5). Then, and only then, has God's love succeeded in its ordained task.

LOVE IS A LAUNCHING PAD

EARLIER WE SAW that God's love creates an atmosphere of peace in which we can find comfort (Ps. 91). God's love is our hiding place, an impregnable fortress against which no attack of any enemy can ultimately succeed.

But God's love is more than a fortress. It is also a launching pad! The Christian must never think that being a recipient of God's love is like winning a gold medal in the Olympic Games. The love of God is never the end of Christian experience. It is the beginning. It isn't the finish line but the starting blocks.

Being loved by God launches us into service and proclamation and generosity. I don't want to unnecessarily offend anyone, but I find it difficult to believe that a person who has been touched by the love of God could ever become a monk. Withdrawal, silence, and solitude are not in the vocabulary of the person who has felt the grasp of God's love.

God's love takes us inside ourselves only long enough for us to marvel that souls so sick with sin could be its recipients. It then drives us outward to those who know nothing of its dynamic qualities.

God's love is a compelling force that thrusts us beyond ourselves and into the lives of others. It was never intended to be a secret, closely guarded by some religious elite. The truth of God's love is not like the cryptic mysteries of a lodge or fraternity. Quite to the contrary, "Christ's love compels us" to proclaim its message to a lost and unlovely world (2 Cor. 5:14). It breaks the silence caused by fear and shatters the shell of passivity.

LOVING THE UNLOVELY

"THERE'S THE 'CAN-MAN,' Daddy," shouted Joanna, our younger daughter.

"I see him, honey."

"Where does he live? He looks so cold," her voice quivering with concern.

"He doesn't live anywhere," I replied.

"You mean he doesn't have a house?" she asked, in stunned disbelief.

"No. No, he doesn't."

At that, her questions ended. Confused, she sat silently in the car, her eyes fixed on the "can-man" with no home.

Walter was a familiar sight to virtually everyone in town. Each day, rain or shine, he could be seen pushing his shopping cart down the street, retrieving aluminum cans as his only means of support. His cart was laden with what few possessions he had. On top was a tiny American flag and on the side a cardboard sign that read, "God loves you."

Occasionally people would stop and give Walter a few dollars or a trash bag full of cans. We bought him some socks. Someone else provided him with a new sleeping bag. Still, Joanna's puzzled look haunted me: "You mean he doesn't have a house?"

A month later we had just concluded a special praise and prayer service one cold Saturday night when Linda, a member of our church, approached me.

"Sam, the Lord wants us to help Walter."

"Fine," I replied. "We'll do what we can."

"You don't understand," said Linda. "He means right now!"

We all loaded into the van and drove out to where we thought he could be found. He was sleeping next to the railroad tracks, beneath the overpass of a busy interstate highway. It was dark, cold, and more than a little scary.

We took Walter some food. Having lost most of his teeth, stew and soft rolls were about the only thing he could chew. It was then that Linda said what all of us knew but didn't have the courage or compassion to admit: "The Lord wants us to feed and clothe and find a home for Walter. Remember what He said: 'I tell you the truth, whatever you did for one of the least of these brothers of mine, you did for me' (Matt. 25:40)."

Linda went immediately to work. With her own money she secured an apartment for two hundred dollars a month, all utilities paid. She utilized a bulletin board at the church, describing both Walter's need and our biblical mandate to meet it. A jar for donations was placed there. It's amazing how much can be done for the poor with mere pocket change! The two hundred dollars was recouped in no time at all.

A can-crusher was purchased and placed near the bulletin board. Soon people began coming to church with a Bible in one hand and a sack full of cans in the other. The kids did their part, crushing the cans each Sunday morning, rejoicing to know that Walter was being fed and housed.

I had never seen Joanna so excited as she was that Sunday when she exclaimed, "Daddy, guess who I saw in church today? The can-man! Walter's here!"

What I've just described goes by different names, depending on whom you ask. Some say it's welfare. Others call it charity. A few insist it's wasteful and useless. After all, so they say, people like Walter don't deserve our assistance. I don't know what word comes to your mind, but I call it mercy. I think God does too.

Walter's story is just one example of what happens when people realize that mercy is something you do. Feeling merciful is essential, but it must bear the fruit of constructive action. Compassion must be concrete and tangible. It must take on the shape and form of Christian people, like Linda, doing for the "least of these brothers" of Jesus what can and must be done.

Why? Because "if anyone has material possessions and sees his brother in need but has no pity on him, how can the love of God be in him? Dear children, let us not love with words or tongue but with actions and in truth" (1 John 3:17–18).

THE MERCY OF THE MASTER

WHEN YOU THINK of Jesus, what is it in Him that you find most attractive? What is it about Him that appeals to you and draws you to Him? Is it His skill as a teacher? Perhaps you are most impressed by His displays of power, or His knowledge, or the authority with which He engaged the religious leaders of His day.

Speaking only for myself, I'm most moved by the compassion and mercy of Jesus. When a man eaten up with leprosy approached Him, Mark tells us that Jesus was so "filled with compassion" that He did what no one else in ancient society dared do. He *touched* him, and the man was cleansed.

Again, it was to Christ's compassion that the father of a demonized boy appealed, wanting to see his son set free. He was (Mark 9:22–27). When Jesus approached the city of Nain, Luke tells us that Jesus came upon a funeral procession. The only son of a widow was about to be buried. When Jesus saw her He felt compassion for her and proceeded to raise her son to life (Luke 7:13–15).

We are all familiar with that occasion on which Jesus fed four thousand people with only seven loaves and a few small fish. But why did He do it? He wasn't the sort of man to perform a miracle simply for its entertainment value. He didn't exploit His powers to increase His following or fame. Matthew tells us that Jesus was filled with *compassion* for the multitude because they had remained so long with Him and had nothing to eat (Matt. 15:32).

And why did Jesus heal the sick, the lame, the blind, and the deaf? Again, because He felt compassion for them (Matt. 14:14).

We are called to be like Christ. So where is our compassion? Where is the mercy of the Master in the lives of His followers? Where is our love for the unlovely?

THE DANGER OF RELIGIOUS COUNTRY CLUBS

THE ANSWER TO this dilemma is complex, but let's focus on what I believe is one of the principal culprits: our distorted concept of the church.

Try to imagine yourself with a broken and bleeding leg, hobbling into the emergency room of your local hospital. The doctors and nurses are all highly educated and skilled practitioners. They are nicely outfitted with freshly pressed uniforms. The equipment is state of the art. The rooms have been refurbished and remodeled.

Yet for all this, you are met at the entrance with reactions of horror and disdain as you overhear the staff say, "Oh, no, not another injured person! Can't we ever get any healthy people in here? I wish we didn't have to waste these new facilities on sick people. If things don't improve soon, I'm going to start looking for a job in another hospital!"

Of course it sounds ludicrous. After all, what are hospitals for if not to help the sick and heal the hurting? But is it any less ludicrous when the distraught, distressed, poor, needy, and sick of soul enter our churches and feel rebuffed for having soiled the high-minded spiritual dignity of the service?

When Jesus promised to build His church He envisioned it not as a museum for saints but as a hospital for sinners. The church is to be a dispensary of mercy, but we have made it a religious country club. Instead of a supportive and sensitive family, one often finds the church to be little more than an ecclesiastical fashion show where people go to convince everyone else of how well they are doing.

People with problems are made to feel sub-Christian. In our

selfishness we view them as little more than an inconvenience. They require more time than we want to give. Talking with them about anything other than the weather might get us entangled in their struggles, so we pass a few pleasantries and quickly find our seat. We rush out after the sermon, more concerned with the football game on television than the person next to us in the pew whose life is shattered.

The apostle John forces us to ask some discomforting questions about ourselves. Can the love of God abide in a person like that? How can we say "God loves me and I love God" when our interaction with the needy is governed by such self-serving, don't-disrupt-my-routine snobbery? Have we deceived ourselves about the love of God? "Dear friends," pleads John, "since God so loved us, we also ought to love one another" (1 John 4:11).

So, what of a practical nature can be done about this? How does one actually love another? How does mercy reveal itself? Let me make just a few suggestions.

First, *start by asking yourself some tough, personal questions.* "Am I the kind of person with whom someone would feel comfortable sharing their struggles? Am I the sort of Christian they would feel encouraged to ask for help? Or am I intimidating? Do I attract those in need or repel them? Does my demeanor say, 'Yes, I *want* to help; yes, I *care*.'? Or do I communicate, apart from words, 'Stay away; you're a disgrace.'?"

What signals do you send out to others? When people in need see you, what comes to their mind? Is it compassion or condemnation? Do they anticipate a reassuring hug or a disdainful look that says, "I can't believe you had the gall to show your face in this church after what you've done."?

Do they sense acceptance and safety, or rejection? Do you advertise yourself as a person who finds others to be an imposition or an opportunity?

Perhaps, then, we each need to begin with this prayer:

> Most merciful heavenly Father, I confess that I've been more committed to preserving my own peace than to binding up the brokenhearted. I have placed a higher pre-

mium on personal convenience than the wounds of Your people. Forgive me. Fill me with the mercy of the Master. Let me love others like the Lord Jesus loves me. Cause my path to cross that of those who need it most.

Be careful, though. Don't pray that prayer unless you mean it, because that's the sort of prayer God delights to answer!

Second, *do something remarkably simple, yet spiritually profound.* Seek out the suffering and pray for them. I didn't say *tell* them you'll pray for them. I said pray for them. That's right. Now. Right where you are. Right where they are.

A few years back I attended a Bible conference in California and came away quite impressed by the people I had met. On the plane trip home I tried to articulate what it was about them that touched me so deeply. I identified three things about their Christianity that I envied and admired.

In the first place, these people had an unashamed, extravagant affection for Jesus. Their love for the Savior was remarkably and refreshingly uninhibited. Another thing that impressed me was the sense of immediacy in their relationship with Him. They walked with Him and talked with Him as you and I might were we to spend an evening together. They lived each moment as if in direct personal communion with a God who truly was present to act and intervene on their behalf.

But what touched me most deeply was their habit of praying for anyone, anywhere, at any time. I've grown tired of hearing people say, upon parting, "I'll pray for you." I've grown tired of saying it myself. These people in California didn't do that. Instead, they prayed! Right there where they were, they prayed. It may have been in line for a hot dog or waiting to enter the restroom or in the middle of the conference room during a break.

Our love for others will never make the impact God desires if it fails to get beyond the comfortable but often empty parting words, "I'll pray for you." So don't say it. Do it.

One day I received a call from a dear lady in our church fellowship who had been suffering from a severe case of shingles (no, not those flat things on your roof). Through tears, she spoke of the gratitude she felt for the ministry of mercy my wife and I had in her life. What had we done to evoke such passion? We had prayed for her. It didn't seem like much, but to her it was everything. "You've been such a blessing," she said. "I can't thank you enough for bearing this burden with me."

That's one of the great things about love. It comes more often in drops than in tidal waves. Little things, like prayer, a well-timed phone call, a card expressing your concern, a gentle hug or pat on the back of someone who feels untouchable, an unsolicited meal, an unannounced visit.

A third thing to do is to *be on the lookout for the "Walters" in your community*. It doesn't take much to mobilize the mercy of a church on behalf of only one homeless person. And remember, your success is not measured by their response but by your initiative. As things turned out, Walter eventually left our city and church. But I'm convinced that, if nothing else was accomplished, he knows something of the love of God that he otherwise would never have known.

Fourth, *seek out the "Walters" in your own church fellowship*. You often need look no further than the person sitting next to you on Sunday morning. Like David, their silent cry is, "No one cares for my soul" (Ps. 142:4, NAS). Look beyond the nice clothes and the crisp smile. God may show you a desperate, dying brother or sister who needs only the reassurance that someone really does care whether they live or die.

It doesn't take much. An encouraging word, a brief prayer, a sincere inquiry into what is going on in their life works wonders. I am reminded of one incident when my wife casually turned to the man sitting next to her one Sunday morning and asked him how his job was progressing. She had no idea that I was counseling his wife, who was threatening him with divorce. Today they are reconciled, and the husband takes every opportunity to remind Ann how much her heartfelt interest in his life meant to him at that critical time of emotional anguish.

Fifth, *mobilize the church youth group to do yard work, minor repairs, and other simple errands for those incapable of caring for themselves*. Don't be put off by the thought that such deeds are too trivial or insignificant. What may appear routine to you is often a crushing burden to those in need.

This is what I meant when I said that God's love never leaves us where we are but leads us to places we've never been. Sometimes it even takes us where we don't want to go! But God's love does more than lead. It transforms. And once you've heard God singing over you, it seems only natural to turn and sing over someone else.

15

Loving Those Who Won't Love Back

ONE BY ONE, they removed their robes and laid them at the feet of a man named Saul. Free to move without restraint, they grasped the instruments of execution and hurled them at the appointed target. These were not mere pebbles tossed in derision, but stones that bruise and break and lacerate . . . and kill.

The rocks cut deeply into Stephen's flesh. Stone shattering bone. "Yes! Do it! Throw another one!"

Stephen fell to his knees. The rockstorm was taking its toll. Yet, amid the shouts of rage, his voice could be heard. With his dying breath he cried, "Lord, do not hold this sin against them" (Acts 7:60).

I don't understand. Do you? Why would a man (indeed, how *could* a man), an *innocent* man, pray for his executioners? Broken, bleeding, dying, Stephen implored God to bless those who so unjustly crushed the life from his body. Why? How?

The answer to the *why?* question is found in the words of Jesus, whom Stephen was determined to obey. "Love your enemies," said Jesus, "and pray for those who persecute you, *that you may be sons of your Father in heaven*" (Matt. 5:44–45, emphasis added).

Stephen loved his enemies because God, Stephen's Father, loves His.

I'll say it again. It bears repeating. God loves His enemies. We are God's sons and daughters. Therefore, we are to love ours. Our relationship to God is displayed when we, like Him, love those who won't love back.

God "causes his sun to rise on the evil and the good, and sends rain on the righteous and the unrighteous" (Matt. 5:45). Our heavenly Father is "kind to the ungrateful and wicked" (Luke 6:35). His mercies rain not only on those who love Him but also on those who complain about getting wet.

"Be merciful," says Jesus, "just as your Father is merciful" (Luke 6:36).

God is the perfect role model. The fact that He is love puts each of us in an unusual position when it comes to our enemies. He blesses those who curse Him. So too should we. How else can you explain Stephen's prayer? How else can you account for his response to those who silenced his request with a flurry of rocks?

But *how* did he do it? Knowing one's duty is one thing. But doing something so seemingly outrageous is altogether another matter.

The answer to the *how?* question must be found in the life-changing impact of being loved by a singing God. Receiving God's love empowers people like Stephen (and you) to do things they otherwise would never so much as dream of doing.

Earlier in Acts it is said of Stephen that he was full of faith and the Holy Spirit and God's grace and power (Acts 6:5, 8). As a result, he "did great wonders and miraculous signs among the people" (Acts 6:8). Greater still was the wonder, the miracle, of *loving his enemies!*

That's how Stephen showed himself to be a son of his Father in heaven (Matt. 5:45). To that degree, he was perfect as his heavenly Father is perfect (Matt. 5:48).

TOUGH LOVE

"TOUGH LOVE" IS a familiar phrase to most people. It refers to firmness when loving someone who is persistently irresponsible. *Love that makes it easy for a person to sin is not love.* Real love sometimes has to be tough on the loved. Tough love calls the loved to account for his actions and to face the consequences of his ill-advised decisions. It may be painful. It may even put the relationship at risk.

But the toughest love of all is the love of one's enemy. Worse than painful, it seems downright silly. It is costly (you may suffer, like Stephen), illogical (by human reasoning), and unrewarding (if all you seek is the approval of others).

What makes it especially tough is that it demands we be different from the world around us. I'm amazed at how willingly people undertake difficult and exacting tasks if they know they will not be alone in their endeavors. But few people are willing to stand apart and cut across the grain of normalcy. Few are willing to walk out of step with the standards of their society. But there is no escaping the fact that Christians are called to be unique. The child of God, says Martyn Lloyd-Jones, " . . . is a man who can never be explained in natural terms. The very essence of the Christian's position is that he is an enigma. There is something unusual, something inexplicable, and something elusive about him from the standpoint of the natural man. He is something quite distinct and apart."[1]

Nothing isolates the Christian from the world quite like the loving of one's enemies. The world says, "Hate them! Avoid them! Best of all, get even with them!"

Jesus says, "Love them. Pray for them. Bless them." Don't expect the world to understand this. Dan Allender reminds us that at best the concept of loving one's enemy is "mocked as pathetic, ignored as irrelevant, or admired as noble, but certainly not seen as practical."[2] That's why you know people must have talked for days about that man Stephen and his dying prayer!

In the previous chapter we talked about how God's love for us is transforming and compelling. It changes us within and drives us out toward others. But what about the "others" who couldn't care less? Are we to love those who won't love back? Are we to love those whose only response is to throw stones? Ask Stephen. Better still, let's ask Jesus.

PERVERTING THE LAW OF LOVE

JESUS SAID:

> You have heard that it was said, "Love your neighbor and hate your enemy." But I tell you: Love your enemies and pray for those who persecute you, that you may be sons of your Father in heaven. He causes his sun to rise on the evil and the good, and sends rain on the righteous and the unrighteous. If you love those who love you, what reward will you get? Are not even the tax collectors doing that? And if you greet only your brothers, what are you doing more than others? Do not even pagans do that? Be perfect, therefore, as your heavenly Father is perfect.
> —MATTHEW 5:43–48

The Old Testament background for what Jesus said is found in Leviticus 19:18. "Do not seek revenge or bear a grudge against one of your people, but love your neighbor as yourself. I am the LORD." The Pharisees, though, couldn't leave well enough alone. They distorted the text in three ways.

First, *they deliberately weakened the standard of the command by omitting the words "as yourself"* (as found in Leviticus 19:18). Perhaps they knew all too well just how much they really did love themselves and realized the impossibility of the task of loving others in like fashion.

Second, *they narrowed the objects of love by insisting that the word "neighbor" referred only to fellow Jews.* Gentiles were excluded, and therefore Gentiles need not be loved. Some Pharisees went so far to insist that only other Pharisees were neighbors! The parable of the Good Samaritan is our Lord's answer to such sinful reasoning. (See Luke 10:25–37.)

Third, and perhaps worst of all, *an addition was made to the love command.* It seemed logical enough that if we are to love our neighbors we should hate our enemies. This is the distortion to which Jesus addresses Himself.

OLD TESTAMENT "HATE"

BUT WE HAVE a problem. What are we to do with all those prayers of *imprecation* in the Old Testament? The term *imprecation* means "the act of invoking or calling down evil or curses upon another person." If you are not familiar with that term, look closely at one of your favorite psalms.

> If only you would slay the wicked, O God! Away from me, you bloodthirsty men! They speak of you with evil intent; your adversaries misuse your name. Do I not hate those who hate you, O LORD, and abhor those who rise up against you? I have nothing but hatred for them; I count them my enemies.
>
> —PSALM 139:19–22

I can't very well exhort you to love your enemies without saying something about David's "hatred" for his. I don't want you blinking at Psalm 139 as if verses 19–22 are a blemish on an otherwise glorious celebration of God.

Don't try to dismiss the problem by insisting such prayers are found only in the Old Testament. Similar sentiments are found in such texts as 1 Corinthians 16:22; Galatians 1:8; 2 Timothy 4:14; Revelation 6:10. And remember, to pray "Thy kingdom come" (Matt. 6:10, KJV) is to invoke divine judgment on those who oppose the reign of God.

What we read in Psalm 139 is not an emotionally uncontrolled outburst by an otherwise sane and compassionate man. Imprecations such as this are found in high poetry and are the product of reasoned meditation (not to mention divine inspiration). They are calculated petitions, not spontaneous explosions of a bad temper.

How, then, do we explain them? And how do we reconcile them with the command of Jesus to love our enemies? Let me make several suggestions that might help.

1. *These prayers are not expressions of personal vengeance.*

In fact, most imprecations are in psalms written by *David,* perhaps the least vengeful man in the Old Testament (consider his dealings with Saul, Nabal, Absalom, Shimei, and others). David never asks that he be allowed to "get even" with or "pay back" his enemies. His prayer is that *God* would act justly in dealing with transgressors. There is a vast difference between vindication and vindictiveness. David's passion was for the triumph of divine justice, not the satisfaction of personal malice.

2. *We also must remember that imprecations are nothing more than human prayers based on divine promises.*

One is simply asking God to do what He has already said He will do. For example, in Matthew 7:21–23, Jesus declares that on the Day of Judgment He will say to hypocrites, "I never knew you. Away from me, you evildoers!" Is it wrong for us to pray that Jesus do precisely that? Is it wrong for us to build a prayer on a promise? "Oh, Lord, cause those to depart from You who do evil" appears to be a perfectly legitimate petition.

3. *Imprecations are expressions provoked by the horror of sin.*

David prayed this way because of his deep sensitivity to the ugliness of evil. Perhaps the chief reason why he wasn't bothered by prayers of imprecation, and we are, is that he was bothered by sin, and we aren't! It is frightening to think that we can stand in the presence of evil and *not* be moved to pray as David did.

4. *The motivation behind such prayers is zeal for God's righteousness, God's honor, God's reputation, and the triumph of God's kingdom.*

Is our willingness to ignore blasphemy and overlook evil due to a deficiency in our love for God and His name? Could our reaction to the imprecatory psalms be traced to the fact that we love men and their favor more than we love God and His?

5. *Another factor to keep in mind is that David, being king, was God's representative on earth.*

Thus an attack on David was, in effect, an attack on God. David's enemies were not his private opponents but adversaries of

God. David's ire is aroused because they "speak of you [God] with evil intent; *your* adversaries misuse *your* name. Do I not hate those who hate *you*, O LORD, and abhor those who rise up against *you?*" (Ps. 139:20–21, emphasis added; cf. Ps. 5:10).

6. *The prayers of imprecation are rarely, if ever, for the destruction of a specific individual.*

They are always used to invoke the destruction of a class or group, namely, "the wicked" or "those who oppose Thee."

7. *All such prayers assume that the wicked are hardened and unrepentant.*

In other words, the psalmist calls for divine judgment against them *so long as* they persist in their rebellion. As we shall see, we love our enemies by praying for their repentance. But if they callously and consistently refuse, our only recourse is to pray that God's judgment be full and fair.

David knows that he needs spiritual protection lest he "hate" God's enemies for personal reasons. That is why he concludes Psalm 139 with the prayer that God purify his motive and protect his heart: "Search me, O God, and know my heart; test me and know my anxious thoughts. See if there is any offensive way in me, and lead me in the way everlasting" (vv. 23–24).

Therefore, when David speaks of "hatred" for those who oppose God's kingdom he is neither malicious nor bitter nor vindictive, nor moved by self-centered resentment. But he most certainly *is* jealous for God's name and firmly at odds with those who blaspheme.

Although it may sound contradictory, we are to "love" those whom we "hate." We love our enemies by doing good to them (Luke 6:27). We love them by providing food when they are hungry and water when they thirst (Rom. 12:20). We love our enemies by blessing them when they persecute and oppress us (Rom. 12:14). We love them by responding to their mistreatment with prayers for their salvation (Luke 6:28).

And yes, we are to "hate" those whom we "love." When they persistently oppose the kingdom of Christ and will not repent, our jealousy for the name of Jesus should prompt us to pray: "O, Lord, wilt Thou not slay the wicked? Vindicate your name,

O Lord, and may justice prevail in the destruction of those who have hardened their hearts in showing spite to your glory."

EVEN PAGANS LOVE PAGANS!

EARLIER I REFERRED to enemy love as "tough" love. There's nothing especially "tough" about loving those who love you back. Even the pagans do that.

Jesus said, "If you love those who love you, what reward will you get? Are not even the tax collectors doing that? And if you greet only your brothers, what are you doing more than others? Do not even pagans do that?" (Matt. 5:46–47).

If God's love enables us to love only those who love us back, why all the fuss and folderol? We're able to do that in the power of the flesh. Why would God bother to sacrifice His Son and send His Spirit to help people do what they are already quite willing and capable of doing? What a colossal waste of divine energy!

Why bother being a Christian at all if the love in our lives is indistinguishable from the love of the non-Christian?

Jesus' appeal to the tax collector is instructive. If you think the IRS has a bad public image, take a look at the first-century "revenoooo-er!"

The Roman empire didn't particularly care how taxes were collected as long as they received their quota. Anything beyond that went directly into the pocket of the tax collector. Needless to say, corruption, thievery, and graft were rampant. The fact that most tax collectors were Jews who served Rome against their own people only added to their already soiled reputation. Being a thief is one thing. To be branded a *traitor* made matters immeasurably worse.

It would be difficult to think of anyone in the ancient Jewish world more despised than the tax collector. By law he was forbidden to have any social interaction with other Jews. He was classified as religiously unclean, along with pigs and lepers. No publican was permitted to give testimony in a court of law. "Tax collectors and sinners" was a standard way of referring to the scum of the earth. (See Matthew 9:10–11; 11:19.)

And yet even these low-life, traitorous outcasts had friends: other tax collectors! Even tax collectors loved other tax collectors. Even pagans greeted other pagans. So how is a follower of Jesus any different if they love only other followers of Jesus?

The practice of treating with kindness those who treat us with kindness is thoroughly secular. There is nothing unique or especially "spiritual" about it. What makes the Christian different is his love for the unloving and the hateful and those who spitefully use and persecute him!

The key word that Jesus uses is "more" (Matt. 5:47). If we love and pray for and treat kindly only those who first do so for us, "what are you doing *more* than others?" In other words, "It is not enough for Christians to *resemble* non-Christians; our calling is to outstrip them in virtue. Our righteousness is to exceed that of the Pharisees . . . and our love is to surpass, to be more than that of the Gentiles."[3]

Overcoming Evil With Good

OUR LOVE IS to be the sort that cannot be explained in purely human terms. It isn't enough simply to refrain from retaliating. We are to bless and pray for those who do us harm. I don't know who said it, but I agree: To return evil for evil is demonic. To return good for good is human. But to return good for evil is divine!

That sentiment is certainly Pauline! The apostle said as much when he told us not to seek vengeance on those who do us dirty. However, many have misunderstood Paul, as if he's saying that all vengeance is evil. But he says no such thing. The reason we are not to seek vengeance is because God has said *He* will (Rom. 12:19), and He can do a much better job of it than we![4]

Enemy love means that instead of responding to evil with evil of our own we are to do good. "In many cases," says Dan Allender, "'doing good' is simply being thoughtful and kind. It boils down to nothing more glamorous than pouring a cup of coffee for someone or warmly greeting them at church and asking about their weekend.

Kindness is the gift of thoughtfulness (Let me look for ways I can serve you.) and compassion (Let me know how I can enter your heart.)."[5]

If you are wanting me to list additional concrete ways to love your enemy, I already have. Read the previous chapter. The way of love is the same. Only the objects have changed. We are to love our enemies in the same way we love our friends.

Paul tells us that in doing so we shall "overcome evil." Dan Allender has explained how this happens in his excellent book *Bold Love.* He points out that when your enemy receives good for evil it *surprises* and *shames* him, both of which have the potential to transform his heart.

The enemy spews out his venom expecting you to respond in kind. Part of the wicked pleasure he derives from being an enemy comes from provoking you to act just as wickedly as he does. "Goodness," though, "trips up the enemy by foiling his battle plans. The enemy anticipates compliance or defensive coldness, harshness, or withdrawal.

The last thing he expects is sustained kindness and steadfast strength. Therefore, when evil is met with goodness, it is apt to respond with either exasperated fury or stunned incredulity. Goodness breaks the spell the enemy tries to cast and renders him powerless."[6]

Goodness, empowered by God's grace, might even open a crack in his hard-shelled heart. Powerless to explain your response in terms of what he knows about human behavior, he is led to acknowledge the life-changing presence of divine love in and through you and your response to his malicious intent. Allender explains the impact of this turning the other cheek:

> The enemy's real pleasure in striking out is the power he enjoys to intimidate and shame. He enjoys inflicting the harm, to some degree, because it gives him a sense of control and the fantasy of being like God. Turning one's cheek to the assault of the enemy demonstrates, without question, that the first blow was impotent and shameful. What was meant to enslave is foiled. Like a boomerang, the

harm swoops around and smacks the back of the head of the one who meant harm. A sorehead may, with the working of the Spirit of God, ask, "Why did I strike that man?" and eventually ask of the one hit, "Why didn't you retaliate?" Again, a measure of astonishment and curiosity is stirred, and the path toward repentance becomes slightly less dim.[7]

Furthermore, goodness shames the enemy. It forces him to look at himself rather than you. When the light of kindness shines back in the face of darkness, the latter is exposed for what it really is. Attention is diverted from the abused to the abuser. The shame he feels upon being "found out" will either harden or soften his heart.

In the very early days of my ministry I was interim pastor of a small church with a history of internal problems. The tiny congregation stood on the brink of yet another split. A congregational meeting was convened at which everyone was given an opportunity to speak his or her mind.

I was young and a bit uncertain of myself, but when the time came I rose to my feet and tried to speak words of encouragement and unity. Suddenly, quite literally in mid-sentence, I was loudly interrupted by a lady who proceeded to accuse me of trying to "steal" the church for my own selfish gain. Unknown to her, or to anyone else present, I had previously accepted an invitation to join the pastoral staff at another church in the same city.

Her words were sharp and cut deeply into my heart. I distinctly remember formulating in my mind a plan of attack to be launched as soon as she quit speaking. Were it not for the grace of God I would have destroyed her (and perhaps, unwittingly, myself as well). But the Spirit silenced my youthful impetuosity. As soon as her verbal barrage ceased, I resumed my comments at precisely the point where I left off. I did not respond to her accusations. I made no attempt at self-defense. It was as if she had never said a word.

The outcome was stunning. My refusal to engage her in the verbal gutter (a decision I attribute wholly to God's grace) served to both silence and shame her. By my declining to respond in kind, her baseless attack was exposed for what it was. Goodness acted like a shield that caused her venom to ricochet back upon her own head. My intent was not to humiliate or harm her in any way, but to lovingly compel her to own up to the motivation of her heart.

For the first time I understood what Paul meant when he said, "If your enemy is hungry, feed him; if he is thirsty, give him something to drink. In doing this, you will heap burning coals on his head" (Rom. 12:20).

"But, Sam, you don't know who *my* enemies are. You have no idea how vile and vengeful and irritating they can be. They take advantage of my goodness; they are unfair. They exploit the fact that I'm a Christian. They constantly embarrass me in front of others, and they lie about me behind my back."

I don't doubt for a moment that what you say is true. I've still got a few enemies like that myself. But if Stephen could love those who viciously stoned him, what excuse do we have for not loving people whose attack on us is admittedly far less grievous?

And what of Jesus Himself? Did He not lovingly pray for His executioners even as they drove iron spikes through His hands and feet? John Stott is surely on the mark: "If the cruel torture of crucifixion could not silence our Lord's prayer for His enemies, what pain, pride, prejudice, or sloth could justify the silencing of ours?"[8]

So the next time someone starts throwing stones in your direction, remember the words of Peter:

> For it is commendable if a man bears up under the pain of unjust suffering because he is conscious of God. But how is it to your credit if you receive a beating for doing wrong and endure it? But if you suffer for doing good and you endure it, this is commendable before God. To this you were called, because Christ suffered for you, leaving you an example, that you should follow in his steps. "He committed no sin, and no deceit was found in his mouth." When they hurled

their insults at him, he did not retaliate; when he suffered,
he made no threats. Instead, he entrusted himself to him
who judges justly.

—1 PETER 2:19–23

16

I Love You, Lord!

T HIS BOOK IS primarily concerned with God's love for us.
But there is no better way to conclude than with our responsibility to love God back. It is our highest and holiest privilege.
We know this on the authority of Jesus Himself.

One day a religious leader walked up to Jesus and asked Him,
"Jesus, in your opinion, what is the single most important thing
for us to do? Of all that God has commanded, what tops the
list?" Our Lord's response deserves our careful attention.

THE GREATEST COMMANDMENT OF ALL

Hearing that Jesus had silenced the Sadducees, the
Pharisees got together. One of them, an expert in the law,
tested him with this question: "Teacher, which is the
greatest commandment in the Law?" Jesus replied: "'Love
the Lord your God with all your heart and with all your
soul and with all your mind.' This is the first and greatest

commandment. And the second is like it: 'Love your neighbor as yourself.' All the Law and the Prophets hang on these two commandments."

—MATTHEW 22:34–40

The Pharisees were delighted that Jesus had silenced (literally, "muzzled") their religious rivals, the Sadducees. (See Matthew 22:23–33.) But they were still frustrated at their own failure to discredit this man from Nazareth. So they decided to have another go at him.

This time they sent an especially brilliant and well-educated man. Matthew calls him an "expert in the law" or "scribe" (Matt. 22:35). Clearly he was an expert in the Mosaic law. He was probably the most learned and astute scholar in their ranks at that time. *If anyone would be a match for Jesus,* they thought, *this guy's the one.*

"Jesus," he asks, "in the lengthy list of God's laws, which is number one?" It wasn't a bad question. The Jews frequently drew distinctions among the laws of Scripture, regarding some as "great" and others "small," some "heavy" and others "light." All were inspired and good and true, but some took precedence over others.

The rabbis had determined there were six hundred thirteen separate letters in the Hebrew text of the Ten Commandments. Likewise, there were six hundred thirteen separate laws in the Pentateuch: two hundred forty-eight positive laws (one, supposedly, for every part of the human body) and three hundred sixty-five negative laws (one for each day of the year). By asking Jesus which was the most important of all, they hoped to trick Him into committing an embarrassing theological error.

"Love God!" Jesus said.

Before you do anything else and in the doing of everything else, "Love God!"

Loving God is preeminent among all virtues. Loving God is the quintessential Christian act. Loving God is paramount.

If our highest and holiest responsibility is to love God, our lowest and most loathsome sin is the failure to do so. Knowing this no doubt prompted the apostle Paul to solemnly declare, "If anyone does not love the Lord—a curse be on him" (1 Cor. 16:22).

Our love for God must be comprehensive. It flows from our heart, from our soul, from our mind, and from our strength. These are not separate faculties on the basis of which we are to build a doctrine of man. Jesus simply means that every molecule of your being is to love God. Your thinking, your feeling, your acting, your speaking, your choosing, all that you are or ever hope to be is designed to love God.

Our love for God must be complete. We are to love Him with "all" our heart and "all" our soul and "all" our mind and "all" our strength! Love for God is to be wholehearted and whole-souled.

I remember well the first time I preached on this passage of Scripture. After the message, a little boy, no more than ten, walked up and complimented me on the sermon. I thanked him and turned to leave, but he wasn't finished.

"Dr. Storms, *how* do I do it?"

"I beg your pardon. How do you do what?"

"How do I love God?"

Leave it to a ten-year-old kid to ruin my Sunday! But he was right. I had spent the good part of fifty minutes telling people how important it was to love God but had failed to tell them *how* to do it! So, how *do* you do it? If I really love God with all my heart, soul, mind, and strength, what will I do? How will I feel? What will others notice about me?

LOVING GOD

I THINK WE can get to the heart of what it means to love God by using an analogy. On several occasions I've mentioned Ann, my wife of twenty-five years. She really is the love of my life. But how would anyone know that's true? Simply telling you I love her won't work. After all, I could be lying. What proof is there? Where is the evidence? How does *she* know that I love her?

If I truly love my wife, there are certain things I will do and feel and say. Likewise, if I truly love God, you will know it in the same way. Consider the following proofs of my love for Ann and, by way of application, the evidence of my love for God.

1. An All-Consuming Passion

First, if I truly and wholeheartedly love her, she will be the *all-consuming passion* of my life. If I love her, there should be a deep, emotional attraction in my heart for her.

As you can see, I strongly disagree with those who say that love is not a feeling but a choice. That isn't to say there's no truth in the assertion that love is what you do. As John Piper points out: "The good in this popular teaching is the twofold intention to show 1) that mere warm feelings can never replace actual deeds of love (James 2:16; 1 John 3:18); and 2) that efforts of love must be made even in the absence of the joy that one might wish were present."[1]

But to argue that love is simply what you do and not also what you feel is irresponsible. It's also boring.

I talked about the role of emotions and feelings in Christian experience in a previous chapter and won't repeat myself here. But let us never forget that whereas love may be more than feelings, it is by no means less than feelings. For true love to exist in its highest and purest form there must be both affection and action.

So let me ask you something. Do you take *delight* in God (Ps. 37:4)? Do you *rejoice* in Him (Phil. 4:4)? Do you seek in God and His presence the *pleasures* that last forever (Ps. 16:11)? When you meditate on His beauty does your heart beat faster? When you reflect on His saving grace do you weep with gratitude?

When I'm with Ann I feel rich and complete and whole. After twenty-five years I still get goose bumps when I see her. I love her. I love God more. No, I don't *always* feel it. I live in a fallen world and in a fallen body. My passions aren't always aflame. I get depressed and feel lonely and sluggish, just like everyone else. But when I do, I pray that God would restore unto me the *joy* of my salvation (Ps. 51:12). I pray that the Spirit would rekindle in my heart the fire of passion for the God who loves me and gave Himself for me. And while I wait, I will diligently *do* what God says.

2. Loyalty and Fidelity

Second, if I truly and wholeheartedly love my wife, she will be the sole recipient of my affection. That is to say, I will be *loyal* to her. I will love *only* her.

I can't very well claim to love her if I'm involved in an extra-marital affair with another woman. The proof of my passion is *fidelity*. Love that isn't loyal isn't love.

If I love God I will be faithful to Him. I will not sleep with other gods. I will not run after another lover. I will not give myself, either in body or soul, to any rival paramour. I will forsake all others and cleave only unto Him. I will not commit idolatry. I will not love money. I will not covet the praise of men above the approval of God.

If I do, I risk provoking God to jealousy. If I violate my love for Ann by giving myself and my affections to someone else, her response will be one of outrage and godly jealousy, and rightly so. Likewise, if I commit spiritual adultery, I inflame the jealous passions of God. "You adulterous people," writes James, "don't you know that friendship with the world is hatred toward God? Anyone who chooses to be a friend of the world becomes an enemy of God" (James 4:4).

God simply will not tolerate a cheating wife. "The fury of God toward His bride is dreadful. He is not going to live meekly with His wife's infidelity. He cannot. He loves her too much, and He has too much self-respect. He will never be content with a bad marriage; He will rage against it until it is changed."[2]

How, then, does my love for Ann show? It is seen in my relentless commitment to be loyal to our marital vows. When we were first saved we, in effect, pledged unto God to be faithful, "and forsaking all others to cleave only unto Him." So remember, you can't love God and play the field.

3. *Loving Protection*

Third, if I truly and wholeheartedly love Ann, I will oppose and resist anything or anyone that seeks to do her harm. I will be diligent to protect her. I will defend her name. What kind of love would it be if I stood by idly and indifferently while her enemies launched a vicious assault?

My love for God reveals itself in the intensity with which I cherish His name. If I really love God, I will cringe each time I hear that precious name used profanely. My love is measured by my reaction to public contempt for His honor. If I were to hear someone defaming my wife, you can be certain that I would rush to her defense. Yet so often we turn a deaf ear to the blasphemous railings against the name of Jesus Christ. He has become little more than a cuss word for many. How can true love do nothing when the Beloved is besmirched?

The psalmist leaves us no alternative: "Let those who love the LORD hate evil" (Ps. 97:10). Why? Because evil is a repudiation of God. Evil, in whatever form, whether in word or deed, is an assault on the Savior. To love God is to hate evil. To love God is to resist and oppose evil without regard for the cost. Love will pay any price to protect the Beloved.

4. *Time Spent Together*

Fourth, if I truly and wholeheartedly love my wife, I will want to *spend time with her*. We don't have to be doing anything special. Just being together is enough.

There was a time when she justifiably questioned the sincerity of my love. We were only dating at the time, but I had already affirmed my love for her. Her doubts were provoked by my habit of taking her in early so that I might return to the fraternity house to eat pizza and play pinball with the guys. She called my hand on it, and she was right.

How much time do you spend with God? Do you visit Him briefly on Sunday, or do you live in His presence every day? How often do you meditate on His word (Ps. 1)? Do you fill your mind with His principles? Do you rehearse in your heart His mighty deeds? Do you enjoy His fellowship?

I enjoy Ann's presence because of who she is. She is gentle. She is smart. She loves me. She satisfies my soul like no other person on this earth.

I enjoy God's presence better still. He is gentler. He is smarter. He loves me more. He satisfies my soul like no other person in the universe. No wonder the psalmist said of God, "You have made known to me the path of life; you will fill me with joy in your presence, with eternal pleasures at your right hand" (Ps. 16:11).

"One thing I ask of the LORD," wrote David, "this is what I seek: that I may dwell in the house of the LORD all the days of my life, to gaze upon the beauty of the LORD and to seek him in his temple" (Ps. 27:4). Now there's a man who loves God!

Dennis Jernigan is one of the most anointed psalmists and worship leaders in the church today. He knows what it means to be loved by God. He also knows what it means to love God. It means:

> When I cannot feel,
> When my wounds don't heal,
> Lord, I humbly kneel,
> Hidden in You.
> Lord, You are my life,
> So I don't mind to die,
> Just as long as I'm
> Hidden in You.
> When I know I've sinned,
> When I should have been
> Crying out, "My God!"
> Hidden in You.
> Lord, I need You now,
> More than I know how,
> So, I humbly bow,
> Hidden in You.
> If I could just sit with You awhile . . .
> If You could just hold me.
> Nothing could touch me,
> Though I'm wounded—though I die!
> If I could just sit with You awhile . . .
> I need You to hold me,
> Moment by moment
> 'Til forever passes by.[3]

5. Communication

Fifth, if I truly and wholeheartedly love Ann, I will talk with her as often as I can. How many times have we heard it said that *communication* is crucial to the success of any relationship? It's true. My love for her is revealed in my effort to open my heart and let her in so that she might share my struggles and hear about my hurts.

My love for her is seen when I make time to listen to what she has to say. She knows I care when even the most important of tasks is set aside to hear what is on her heart or what filled her day.

So, how is your prayer life? Your love for God is measured by the depth of your communion with Him in prayer. I've heard it many times from embittered wives: "How can he say he loves me when he never talks to me?" That's a good question. How can you say you love God when you so rarely talk to *Him?*

How can we say we love God when we so rarely *listen* to what *He* has to say? The next time you pray, shut up. You read it right. Shut up . . . and listen. Let God share *His* heart with you. Mutual, two-way communication is the lifeblood of every true love affair. So tell the Lord what you need, what you're thinking, what scares you. Then hush, and let Him soothe your soul with His own words of tender love.

6. *Obedience*

Sixth, if I truly and wholeheartedly love my wife, I will seek to do those things that please her and increase her joy. I will do my best to take out the trash before our kitchen becomes an odorous obstacle course. I will remember to remember our anniversary. I will guard my lips against impetuous and heartless criticism.

How, then, do we love God? Jesus said it best: "If you love me, you will obey what I command" (John 14:15). That pretty much settles it, don't you think! If you have any lingering doubts, listen again: "Jesus replied: 'If anyone loves me, he will obey my teaching. My Father will love him, and we will come to him and make our home with him. He who does not love me will not obey my teaching. These words you hear are not my own; they belong to the Father who sent me'" (John 14:23–24).

7. *Boast in God*

Seventh, if I truly and wholeheartedly love Ann, I will brag on her to others. I will boast of her beauty and rave about her godly life. I will be quick to tell the world how wonderful a mother she is to our two daughters. I will be careful never to demean her or question her worth in public (or private).

And if I truly love God I will *brag on Him!* That's right. *Our boast is in God!* "Give thanks to the LORD, call on his name; make known among the nations what he has done" (1 Chron. 16:8). That sure sounds like bragging to me. Tell the world how great He is. Boast aloud of His goodness. "Glory [literally, 'boast'] in his holy name" (1 Chron. 16:10).

The person who truly loves God will praise God. The lover of God will ache with anticipation for those times of corporate worship when, with the believing community, she can raise her heart and voice to magnify the beauty of the Lord. Here is the passion of the lover of the Lord: "How lovely is your dwelling place, O LORD Almighty! My soul yearns, even faints, for the courts of the LORD; my heart and my flesh cry out for the living God. . . . Blessed are those who dwell in your house; they are ever praising you" (Ps. 84:1–2, 4).

8. *Speak of Your Love*

Eighth, if I truly and wholeheartedly love my wife, I will tell her so! The dumbest thing any man could ever say is, "Oh, I don't need to tell her I love her. She knows it by my actions." Nonsense! Love is more than merely "saying so," but it certainly isn't less than that!

Wives have every reason to doubt their husband's love if they never hear them say so. Perhaps I go a bit overboard on this one, but I tell Ann that I love her at least a half-dozen times a day. But I've never heard her complain. She's never told me to shut up. She's never given me the slightest indication that it's repetitive or irritating.

I have to confess, though, that telling Ann how much I love her hasn't always been easy. When we first began dating in college I frequently told *others* how much I cared for her. I would return to my fraternity house after a date and tell my roommate how wonderful she was and how I was sure I could never love another.

But when we were together, I found it difficult to say *to* her what I freely said *about* her in the presence of friends. I never had a problem doting on her when others were around. But when it came time to look Ann in the face and say, "*I* love *you*," my stomach knotted up, my throat contracted, my mouth became a desert, and I generally made a fool of myself.

Why? Because we fear letting our real feelings be known to

the person for whom we have them. We are afraid they won't feel about us the way we feel about them. The prospect of not being loved back is terrifying. No one wants to be left emotionally stranded. Putting ourselves in such a vulnerable position with someone whose response we aren't sure we can trust is too scary for most people.

But that's no longer a problem. I still tell others how much I love my wife. I talk *about* her every chance I get (as you can tell from reading this book). But I'm not afraid to tell her face to face. After twenty-five years of marriage we've grown to trust each other. The fear is gone. Our love has deepened, and we feel free to share our innermost feelings and thoughts.

Now try to think of this in terms of your relation to God. To tell others *about* God is certainly good. It's important for us to join with other believers and sing what I call "third-person" praise: "*He* is good and gracious," and "We love *Him*." But there's something extraordinarily special about "second-person" praise. Third-person praise is telling others *about* God, about *Him*. Second-person praise is telling God Himself. It's one thing to say, "We love God." It's something else and altogether more intimate to say, "God, *I* love *You*."

The current revival of praise and worship in the evangelical community bears witness to this. Have you noticed how many of the praise songs and choruses that are most popular today are phrased in the first person? Declarations such as, "*I* worship *You*," "*I* love *You*," "*I* adore *You*," "*You* are *my* all in all," engage our deepest and most personal feelings in a way that "*We* love *Him*" never could.

I suspect this is why some people are still resistant to the new worship music. They are uncomfortable in speaking so directly and passionately *to* God of their feelings for Him, especially in the presence of others who might overhear.

So let me ask you a question: How often do you tell God that you love Him? Is your heart filled only with detached and potentially impersonal "third-person" praise? Or do you turn your eyes toward heaven, look your Lord in the face, and say, "O dear Father, *I* love *You*"? Go ahead, try it. He'll like it!

This book is about the singing God. It is about the God who takes such delight in His children that He sings over them in love. I hope and pray you can hear His songs of affection for you. I also hope and pray you'll sing one to Him.

Epilogue

$\mathcal{T}$HE LITTLE BOY wanted nothing more than to live in the presence of the Great King. He especially liked taking walks with Him. Wherever they went he felt safe and secure, as if enveloped by a warm blanket. He knew no fear, confident that the King could ward off any attack of the enemy.

Their time together now seemed somehow special, for the King was also his Father. As they travelled together the little boy held tightly to his Father's hand. His Father's grip was tighter still, but never hurtful. Whether in gardens or on hilltops, in valleys or while crossing a bridge, their fingers were firmly intertwined.

The little boy knew now that his Father loved him. He knew now that such love would never die. His heart took comfort as he listened to his Father hum, then sing, of His love for His child.

One day, quite suddenly and without warning, the Father reached down and picked up the little boy. He held him closely to His breast and hugged him ever so affectionately. Tears of joy filled his Father's eyes. The song on His lips grew louder and more intense as He showered His child with kisses and tender love.

Then He gently placed him back on the ground, their hands again locked in love as they resumed their walk together.

My prayer is that, having read this book, you know precisely what the little boy was feeling. You've always been told that God loves you. You've always hoped that He did. But you needed to be picked up and embraced and to feel in the depths of both body and soul what your mind had been telling you all along was true.

The little boy's assurance of the Father's love was doubly reinforced by that momentary, effusive display of affection. My prayer is that this book has in some small way renewed in you the selfsame joy of being loved, of being enjoyed, of having God, your Father, sing over you.

Can you hear Him singing?

Appendix A

Abba! Father!

$\mathcal{W}$HAT COMES TO mind when you hear the word "God?" What is your concept of the Creator?

I've talked with people who relate to God as if He were something of a *coach*. There's no real relationship, at least not on a personal level. Joining the church is like making the team. When God does choose to communicate, it isn't with soft-spoken words of loving encouragement but with an angry shout of "Run faster! Jump higher! Two more laps!" One's responsibility is to train hard, perform well on game day, and perhaps be fortunate enough to get a slap on the seat and a perfunctory "Nice job."

Others think of God more as a *teacher*. To them, being a Christian means studying harder, learning more, memorizing doctrines and texts of Scripture, and then regurgitating it all on test day. The important thing is getting all "*A*s" and graduating to the next "grade" of spirituality. God's primary role is to make sure we spell His name right and assign detention when we misbehave.

Then there are those for whom God is a *boss*. Getting a good job in the kingdom is priority one. Christians are just so many employees who are responsible for getting to work on time and putting in a solid eight hours. God is there principally to fill out performance reports and to decide who gets a raise, who gets a vacation, and who gets fired!

To speak to such people about God being their *Father* can be risky. It not only doesn't compute, it confuses and angers them. The reason isn't hard to understand. The very word *Father* may yet evoke the image of an abusive bully with a stick in his hand. Others think only of a void in their home, the never-present father whose selfish disregard for their needs hurts as much now as it did then.

It may be that on hearing the word *Father* you smell the stench of alcohol. Perhaps you feel the abusive hand, groping where it should not be, soon after you'd fallen asleep. God knows. He is keenly aware of how difficult it is for you to entrust your soul to another when your former wounds have yet to heal.

But He is a Father unlike any other. His love transcends that of even the most caring earthly parent. Won't you allow Him to describe His love for you and the potential for your relationship together? It's all wrapped up in one word. Jesus used it. So can we.

FATHER LOVES BEST

Jesus always spoke of God as "My Father," whether as a formal designation or an address to God in prayer. Closer study reveals that Jesus used this address in *all* His prayers, with one exception. From the cross He cried, "My God, my God, why have you forsaken me?" (Mark 15:34).

The reason for this sole exception is not simply that Jesus was drawing from an Old Testament text in which the form of address was already supplied. (See Psalm 22:2.) His cry, "My God," rather than "My Father," was a consequence of the judgment to which He was being subjected.

As He hung on Calvary's tree for sinners, Jesus evidently regarded His relationship to God as penal and judicial, not paternal and filial. But in the other twenty-one instances where Jesus prayed, He always addressed God as His Father.

In the Old Testament, God was referred to in many ways, but rarely as *Father*. The word is used of Him only fifteen times, apart from several texts in which God is compared with an earthly father. (See Psalm 103:13; Proverbs 3:12; Jeremiah 31:20.)

In seven instances God is conceived as *Father of the nation Israel* (Deut. 32:6; Isa. 63:16; 64:8; Jer. 31:9; Mal. 1:6; 2:10). In five other passages God is called the *Father of the king* in fulfillment of one element of the Davidic covenant (2 Sam. 7:14; 1 Chron. 17:13; 22:10; 28:6; Ps. 89:26). God is called *Father of the orphaned* in a song of praise for His tenderness (Ps. 68:5). In two cases where "my Father" is used as an *invocation to God in prayer*, it is a prayer, not of any single individual, but of the nation collectively (Jer. 3:4, 19).

Judging from these passages, it was anything but characteristic of Old Testament spiritual life to refer to God as Father in personal prayer and communion. That depth of intimacy with the Almighty was rare indeed.

Yet, aside from the exception noted above, this is precisely what our Lord Jesus Christ did *every time* He prayed!

Still more significant is the fact that he used the word *Abba* when referring to the Father (Mark 14:36; most scholars agree that the Aramaic term *abba* lies back of the Greek *pater*). *Abba* was a term used in Judaism to express the intimacy, security, and tenderness of a family relationship. More specifically, it was a word that tiny children used to address their fathers. Of course, it didn't preclude courtesy and respect. But above all it was an expression of warm affection and trust.

We read in the Talmud that when a child is weaned "it learns to say 'abba' (daddy) and 'imma' (mommy)."[1] Again, the point is that "there is no analogy at all in the whole literature of Jewish prayer (specifically the Palestinian Judaism of our Lord's day) for God being addressed as *Abba*."[2]

Joachim Jeremias argues that "to the Jewish mind it would have been disrespectful and therefore inconceivable to address God with this familiar word. For Jesus to venture to take this step was something new and unheard of. He spoke to God like a child to its father: simply, inwardly, confidently. Jesus' use of *abba* in addressing God reveals the heart of His relationship with God."[3]

When the apostle Paul wrote to the Roman (8:15–16) and Galatian (4:6) Christians, saying that we as God's children may likewise address our Father in this way, the depth of that intimacy with God secured for us by the cross of Christ becomes joyfully evident.

Just think of it! The one true God who beckons you with the promise of perfect love is none other than your Father, *Abba!* You need not fear an abusive grasp or a stiff-armed rejection. He longs to embrace you, to relieve your fears, to soothe the wounds inflicted by those who exploited your weakness.

There is joy unspeakable in this truth. How can I describe the comfort and thrill in knowing that the One into whose arms we rush and, as it were, on whose lap we sit, is our Father, our "Daddy?" He, in the crook of whose arm we repose, is our *Abba*. No earthly father ever embraced his child with such affection and tenderness as does He who cradles you with a song.

Appendix B

Does God Love Himself?

*W*HY DOES GOD LOVE YOU? You had better sit down before I answer that question. Are you comfortable? Here goes. *God loves you because God loves Himself.* Again, God loves you because God loves Himself. God is committed to your best interests because He is first and foremost committed to His own. God loves us because in doing so He glorifies Himself.

It sounds pretty selfish, doesn't it? Are you offended? Are you repulsed? After all, how can God love us to the fullest if He is committed to loving Himself that way?

I was greatly helped in understanding this by something J. I. Packer wrote in his book *Hot Tub Religion*. He said:

> The only answer that the Bible gives to questions that begin: "Why did God . . . ?" is: "For his own glory."[1]

Everything God does is for His own glory. Everything God permits is for His own glory. Everything God pursues is for His own glory. When God acts it is for the sake of His name.

Why did God create and redeem a people who would be called by His name? He did it for His own glory (Isa. 43:7).

Why did God raise up Pharaoh and harden his heart? He did it to make known His glory (Exod. 14:4, 18).

Why did God intervene to deliver Israel from bondage in Egypt? He did it for the sake of His own name (Ezek. 20:9).

Why did God decline to destroy Israel in the wilderness after her repeated rebellions? He did it for the sake of His own name (Ezek. 20:21–22; Ps. 106:6–8).

Why did God choose not to abandon Israel in Babylon, though she certainly was deserving of it? Listen to God explain His motivation:

> For my own name's sake I delay my wrath; *for the sake of my praise* I hold it back from you, so as not to cut you off. . . . *For my own sake, for my own sake, I do this.* How can I let *myself* be defamed? *I will not yield my glory to another.*
> —ISAIAH 48:9, 11, EMPHASIS ADDED; CF. EZEKIEL 36:22–23

Why does God guide us in paths of righteousness? He does it "for his name's sake" (Ps. 23:3).

Why does God forgive us our sin? He does it for the sake of His name (Ps. 25:11).

Why did Jesus endure the shame and suffering of the cross? He did it to glorify the name of His Father, our God (John 12:27–28; Phil. 2:6–10).

Why did God elect us in Christ before the foundation of the world and redeem us by His blood? He did it "to the praise of His glorious grace" (Eph. 1:6, 12).

Why did God give us His Spirit as a deposit guaranteeing our inheritance? He did it "to the praise of His glory" (Eph. 1:14).

Why does Jesus command us to do good works? He does it so that men "may see your good deeds and praise your Father in heaven" (Matt. 5:16).

Why are we told to use our spiritual gifts in the strength that God supplies? It is "so that in all things God may be praised through Jesus Christ" (1 Pet. 4:11).

Why is Jesus planning on returning to this earth? What does He intend to accomplish? He is coming back primarily "to be glorified in his holy people and to be marveled at among all those who have believed" (2 Thess. 1:10).

Have we settled that point? Does anyone wish to dispute that the only answer to the question, "Why did God . . . ?" is: "For His own glory"? If you still have doubts, there are many more texts just like these. But I see no need to list them at length.

What this means is that God delights in His own glory above all else. He is at the center of His own affections. The love of God's life is God. He values Himself and His own name above everything and everyone else.

To love someone is to treat that person as valuable. It is to regard them highly and to act on their behalf and welfare. Although we should be cautious in saying that God "must" do this or that, of one thing I am certain: God *must* value Himself supremely. God *must* love Himself preeminently. John Piper explains:

> God has many other goals in what He does. But none of them is more ultimate than this. They are all subordinate. God's overwhelming passion is to exalt the value of His glory. To that end He seeks to display it, to oppose those who belittle it, and to vindicate it from all contempt. It is clearly the uppermost reality in His affections. He loves His glory infinitely.[2]

This is just another way of saying that *God loves Himself* infinitely. Are you turned off by this? Does it seem arrogant and egotistical of God to be preeminently concerned with His own glory? Probably so. The reason why isn't difficult to ascertain. We intuitively recoil from people who are always seeking their own glory.

Suppose a man moves to your city and joins your church and is asked why he did so. He answers, "I have come here looking for praise and glory and honor and recognition for myself, and your city and church strike me as the most effective place and people through which to achieve my end." That's not the kind of man you'd be inclined to invite to lunch after services on Sunday morning!

We don't like the idea of a soldier enlisting in the Army just to win medals or a Boy Scout assisting an elderly lady just to get merit badges. We turn away in disgust from the self-centered athlete who plays solely for personal acclaim or from the scholar who reminds us regularly of his academic credentials.

So, how does *God* escape our disdain? How can we be asked to admire God for doing what we condemn in others?

My answer comes as a question. "Is it right to cherish and exalt that which is supremely valuable?" I'm sure you said *yes*. Both the Bible and common sense tell us that we are to value what is most valuable and to honor what is most honorable.

Now, let's suppose a fire breaks out in Mrs. Wilson's home. She awakens to the smell of smoke and realizes she has but a few seconds to grab one thing before the house collapses on top of her. So she picks up her Siamese cat and dashes for the door, leaving behind her six-month-old infant girl to die of smoke inhalation.

All of us are justifiably outraged by Mrs. Wilson's choice. That she would place more value on a cat than a child is reprehensible and unrighteous. Thankfully, she's only a hypothetical lady in an illustration. But she does effectively highlight the universal principle that we are morally required to cherish what is most valuable.

Who is the supremely valuable being in the universe? It is *God*, of course. *God* is the preeminently worthy One and the most honorable being in existence. That is why we worship only Him and ascribe all glory to His name (Exod. 20:3–4).

Now follow carefully what Packer says:

> If it is right for man to have the glory of God as his goal, can it be wrong for God to have the same goal? If man can have no higher purpose than God's glory, how can God? If it is wrong for man to seek a lesser end than this, it would be wrong for God, too. The reason it cannot be right for

man to live for himself, as if he were God, is because he is not God. However, it cannot be wrong for God to seek His own glory, simply because He is God. Those who insist that God should not seek His glory in all things are really asking that He cease to be God. And there is no greater blasphemy than to will God out of existence.[3]

How could we describe God as righteous and good if He ever failed to pursue and preserve that which is supremely valuable and of greatest worth? We couldn't! God "must" take ultimate delight in His own glory or He would be unrighteous.

"For it is right to take delight in a person in proportion to the excellence of that person's glory."[4] And if God were to commit an unrighteous act He would cease to exist as God.

Don't you now see that for God to fail or refuse to value Himself preeminently would implicate Him in the sin of idolatry? We must remember that the rules of humility that govern creatures do not apply to the Creator. If God were ever to act in such a way that He did not seek His own glory He would be saying that something more valuable than Himself exists, and that is a lie. Worse still, it is idolatrous.

The reason it is sinful for us to seek our own glory is because there is something more valuable and important than ourselves. We are but creatures.

For the same reason it is righteous for God to seek His own glory because nothing is more important or more worthy than God. He is the Creator.

To sum up: *God loves Himself infinitely*. His own glory is the principal focus of all His energy and efforts.

It follows from this that everything He does is designed to win praise for that glory from His people. Says Piper:

All the different ways God has chosen to display His glory in Creation and Redemption seem to reach their culmination in the praises of His redeemed people. God governs the world with glory precisely that He might be admired, marveled at, exalted, and praised. The climax of His happiness is the delight He takes in the echoes of His excellence in the praises of the saints.[5]

How, then, can He be a God of love? If God loves Himself above all others, how can He love others at all? If He is passionately committed to doing everything for His own sake, how can He be passionately committed to ours?

And that *is* the thesis of this book—that God passionately and fervently loves *us*.

So again, if God is for Himself, how can He be for us? Here's where things get *really* interesting.

If God were to cease loving Himself supremely He would cease being God, for He will have committed an idolatrous act. If this were to occur, *we* are the ones who stand to lose most. "For where can we go when our God has become unrighteous? Where will we find a Rock of integrity in the universe when the heart of God has ceased to value supremely the supremely valuable? Where shall we turn with our adoration when God Himself has forsaken the claims of infinite worth and beauty?"[6]

We are now prepared to ask two questions, the answers to which, I hope, will make sense of all that has preceded.

First, what is the most loving thing that God could do for you? John Piper puts it like this: "What could God give us to enjoy that would prove Him most loving? There is only one possible answer: *Himself!* If He withholds Himself from our contemplation and companionship, no matter what else He gives us, He is not loving."[7]

Now for the second question. "*What do we all do when we are given or shown something beautiful or excellent?* We *praise* it!"[8]

In fact, our joy in the gift is incomplete *until* we praise it. I agree with C. S. Lewis, who said:

> I think we delight to praise what we enjoy because the praise not merely expresses but completes the enjoyment; it is its appointed consummation. It is not out of compliment that lovers keep on telling one another how beautiful they are; the delight is incomplete till it is expressed.[9]

What this means is that if God loves us, and He does, He will do two things: First, *He will give Himself to us*. He is Himself the greatest gift. Second, *He will work to secure from us the praise of His glory*, "not because He needs to shore up some weakness in Himself or compensate for some deficiency, but because He loves us and seeks the fullness of our joy that can be found only in knowing and praising Him, the most magnificent of all Beings."[10] That is why if God is going to be for us He must be for Himself. Piper puts it like this:

> God is the one Being in all the universe for whom seeking His own praise is the ultimately loving act. For Him, self-exaltation is the highest virtue. When He does all things "for the praise of His glory," He preserves for us and offers to us the only thing in all the world that can satisfy our longings. God is for us! And the foundation of this love is that God has been, is now, and always will be, for Himself.[11]

Let me try to clarify all this with a brief summary. My point has been that if God is going to love us to the fullest, if God is going to seek our eternal happiness and welfare, He must be committed above all else to the pursuit of His own glory. He must do whatever is best suited to magnify His own name and to advertise His own glory. In other words, if God is going to love us He must first love Himself. The most loving thing that God can do for you is to love Himself preeminently.

In fact, since God is the most honorable and praiseworthy being in the universe, it would be idolatry if He failed to pursue His own glory above all else. He would be guilty of honoring as God something or someone other than God.

Now, how would a God like this go about loving us? Would it not be by providing us with the highest good possible? And is not *God Himself* the highest good? In other words, if God really loves us, He must work to bring us into the enjoyment of who He is and thereby win from our hearts praise for Himself. He must do everything in His infinite power to lead us into praise and honor of His name. By winning for Himself your worship as the God of all glory, you experience the greatest possible satisfaction, namely, *enjoying God*. And God is glorified by your enjoyment of Him. Or, as John Piper so often puts it, *God is most glorified in you when you are most satisfied in Him.*

Thus, for God to seek His own glory and for God to seek your good are not separate or antithetical endeavors. That is because God is most glorified in us (there's His glory) when we are most satisfied in Him (there's our good). Therefore, if God were not committed *first* to His own glory, He would not be *at all* committed to our good.

Our highest good is in the enjoyment of God. God's highest good is in being enjoyed. Thus, for God to work for your enjoyment of Him (that's His love for you) and for His glory in being enjoyed (that's His love for Himself) are not properly separable. Glory to God!

Notes

CHAPTER 1
WHY THIS BOOK WAS WRITTEN

1. Joni Eareckson Tada, *Secret Strength* (Portland, OR: Multnomah Press, 1988), 348.
2. Ibid.
3. Ibid., 349.

CHAPTER 2
GOD'S PASSION FOR HIS PEOPLE

1. Sherwood Eliot Wirt, *Jesus, Man of Joy* (San Bernardino, CA: Here's Life Publishers, 1991).
2. Ibid., 22.
3. This is the thesis of John Piper's book, *The Pleasures of God: Meditations on God's Delight in Being God* (Portland, OR: Multnomah Press, 1991).
4. O. Palmer Robertson, *The Books of Nahum, Habakkuk, and Zephaniah* (Grand Rapids, MI: Eerdmans, 1990), 340.

CHAPTER 3
IS GOD A BARITONE OR BASS?

1. Warren Wiersbe, *Real Worship* (Nashville, TN: Oliver Nelson, 1986), 137.
2. Quoted in Roland Bainton, *Here I Stand: A Life of Martin Luther* (Nashville, TN: Abingdon, 1950), 341.
3. Ibid.
4. Ibid., 343.
5. Quoted by Richard D. Dinwiddie in "When You Sing Next Sunday, Thank Luther," *Christianity Today*, October 21, 1983, 19–20.
6. Ibid., 21.
7. Piper, *The Pleasures of God,* 187.
8. Ibid., 197–99.

CHAPTER 4
THE OBSCENITY OF THE CROSS

1. The best treatment of the ethical problem entailed by this command is provided by Thomas McComiskey in his commentary on Hosea in *The Minor Prophets: An Exegetical and Expository Commentary,* vol. 1, *Hosea, Joel, and Amos,* ed. by Thomas Edward McComiskey (Grand Rapids, MI: Baker Book House, 1992), 11–17.
2. "Pseudo-Manetho," as quoted by Martin Hengel in *Crucifixion* (Philadelphia, PA: Fortress Press, 1977), 9.
3. N. Haas, "Anthropological Observations on the Skeletal Remains from GIV at HA-Mivtar," *Israel Exploration Journal* 20, 1970, 58.
4. John Calvin, *A Harmony of the Gospels, Matthew, Mark & Luke,* vol . 3, translated by A. W. Morrison (Grand Rapids, MI: Eerdmans, 1972), 194.
5. Quoted by Martin Hengel, *Crucifixion,* 2.

CHAPTER 5
ORPHANS TO HEIRS

1. Piper, *The Pleasures of God*, 271.
2. J. I. Packer, *Knowing God* (Downers Grove, IL: InterVarsity Press, 1973), 195.
3. Ibid., 196.

CHAPTER 6
A CLEAN SLATE

1. Charles H. Spurgeon, *The Treasury of David*, vol. 1b (Grand Rapids, MI: Zondervan, 1976), 82.
2. Jerry Bridges, *Transforming Grace: Living Confidently in God's Unfailing Love* (Colorado Springs, CO: Navpress, 1991), 40.
3. Spurgeon, *The Treasury of David*, 82.
4. The complete story is told by Jackie Pullinger in her book, *Chasing the Dragon* (Ann Arbor, MI: Servant Books, 1980), 70–73.
5. Ibid., 71.
6. Dan B. Allender and Tremper Longman, *Bold Love* (Colorado Springs, CO: Navpress, 1992), 43.

CHAPTER 7
HOW LONG WILL LOVE WAIT?

1. C. John Miller and Barbara Miller Juliani, *Come Back, Barbara* (Grand Rapids, MI: Zondervan, 1988).
2. Ibid., 10.
3. Kenneth E. Bailey, *Poet and Peasant and Through Peasant Eyes: A Literary-Cultural Approach to the Parables in Luke* (Grand Rapids, MI: Eerdmans, 1976), 161–62.
4. Phil Davis, *The Father I Never Knew: Finding the Perfect Parent in God* (Colorado Springs, CO: Navpress, 1991), 87.

CHAPTER 8
WHEN LOVE HURTS

1. Philip E. Hughes, *A Commentary on the Epistle to the Hebrews* (Grand Rapids, MI: Eerdmans, 1977), 528.
2. Malcolm Muggeridge, *A Twentieth Century Testimony* (Nashville, TN: Thomas Nelson, 1978), 35.
3. J. I. Packer, *Rediscovering Holiness* (Ann Arbor, MI: Servant Publications, 1992), 215.
4. "How Firm a Foundation." No copyright listed.

CHAPTER 9
SINGING IN A CESSPOOL

1. Donald A. Carson, *How Long, O Lord? Reflections on Suffering and Evil* (Grand Rapids, MI: Baker Book House, 1990), 73.
2. Ronald Allen, *Praise: A Matter of Life and Breath* (Nashville, TN: Thomas Nelson, 1980), 152.
3. Ibid., 155.
4. Packer, *Rediscovering Holiness*, 217.
5. Ibid.
6. "In the Garden" by Austin Miles. Copyright © 1912 by Hall-Mack. Renewed

1940 by The Rodeheaver Co. (A Div. of WORD MUSIC). All right reserved. Used by permission.

7. As told in *Renewal,* no. 185, October 1991, 4.

CHAPTER 10
A LOVE YOU CAN COUNT ON

1. Spurgeon, *Treasury of David,* 107.

2. Piper, *The Pleasures of God,* 208.

3. The interview was conducted by Patrick B. McGuigan and printed in *The Daily Oklahoman,* December 19, 1991.

4. Ibid.

CHAPTER 11
LOVE'S VICE GRIP!

1. The complete story is told by Jackie Pullinger in her book, *Chasing the Dragon* (Ann Arbor, MI: Servant Books, 1980), 15–19.

2. Ibid.

3. J. W. Alexander, *God Is Love* (Carlisle: Banner of Truth Trust, 1985, previously published in 1860), 45.

4. J. I. Packer, *Your Father Loves You,* compiled and edited by Jean Watson (Wheaton, IL: Harold Shaw Publishers, 1986), entry for September 10.

5. "O Love That Will Not Let Me Go." No copyright listed. Although we can't be certain of the timing of the hymn's composition, the evidence points to this occasion. See Kenneth W. Osbeck, *101 Hymn Stories* (Grand Rapids, MI: Kregel Publications, 1982), 189–91.

6. Piper, *The Pleasures of God,* 194–95.

7. Ibid., 195.

8. "How Firm a Foundation."

CHAPTER 12
FEELING LOVED

1. D. Martyn Lloyd-Jones, *Preaching and Preachers* (Grand Rapids. MI: Zondervan, 1971), 95.

2. Ibid., 94.

3. Jack Hayford, *A Passion for Fullness* (Dallas, TX: Word Books, 1990), 31.

4. None of this is intended to deny the validity of the spiritual gift of discerning of spirits, which, on any definition, requires a subjective element when used. (See 1 Corinthians 12:10.) Nor do I wish to deny the validity of subjective impressions imparted by the Holy Spirit for purposes of guidance. (See Acts 13:2; 16:6–7.)

5. John Piper, *Desiring God* (Portland, OR: Multnomah Press, 1986), 225. I consider this book to be the most important and insightful volume of the last decade. I am deeply indebted to John Piper for his work and even more so for his passionate desire for God.

CHAPTER 13
THE JOY OF RECEIVING GOD'S LOVE

1. "O Lord, Your Tenderness" by Graham Kendrick. Copyright 1986 by Kingsway Thankyou Music/Admin. in North, South, and Central America by Integrity's Hosanna! Music/ASCAP. All right reserved. International copyright secured. Used by permission. c/o Integrity Music, Inc., P.O. Box 851622, Mobile, AL 36685.

2. John Murray, *The Epistle to the Romans* (Grand Rapids, MI: Eerdmans, 1971), 165.

3. E. H. Gifford, *The Epistle of St. Paul to the Romans* (Minneapolis, MN: The James Family Publishing, 1977), 112.

4. Charles Hodge, *Commentary on the Epistle to the Romans* (Grand Rapids, MI: Eerdmans, 1974), 135.

5. Packer, *Knowing God,* 107.

6. W. R. Moody, *The Life of D. L. Moody* (New York: Fleming H. Revell, 1900), 149.

7. Packer, *Knowing God,* 107.

8. D. A. Carson, *A Call to Spiritual Reformation: Priorities From Paul and His Prayers* (Grand Rapids, MI: Baker Book House, 1992), 191.

9. Andrew T. Lincoln, Word Biblical Commentary, *Ephesians* (Dallas: Word Books, 1990), 213.

ADDENDUM
FELT LOVE IN THE LIFE OF SARAH EDWARDS

1. The complete text of Sarah Edward's testimony may be found in *The Works of Jonathan Edwards,* Volume 1 (Carlisle, PA: Banner of Truth Trust, 1979 [1834]), pp. lxii–lxx.

CHAPTER 14
THE SINGING SAINT

1. John R. W. Stott, *The Epistles of John* (Grand Rapids, MI: Eerdmans, 1976), 164.

CHAPTER 15
LOVING THOSE WHO WON'T LOVE BACK

1. D. Martyn Lloyd-Jones, *Studies in the Sermon on the Mount* (Grand Rapids, MI: Eerdmans, 1974), 312.

2. Allender and Longman, *Bold Love,* 207.

3. John R. W. Stott, *Christian Counter-Culture: The Message of the Sermon on the Mount* (Downers Grove, IL: InterVarsity Press, 1978), 121.

4. See Allender's excellent treatment of this subject in *Bold Love,* 183–226.

5. Ibid., 211.

6. Ibid., 216.

7. Ibid., 224–25.

8. Stott, *Christian Counter-Culture,* 119.

CHAPTER 16
I LOVE YOU, LORD!

1. Piper, *Desiring God,* 93.

2. Tim Stafford, *The Sexual Christian* (Wheaton, IL: Victor Books, 1989), 79.

3. "If I Could Just Sit With You Awhile" by Dennis Jernigan. Copyright © 1991 by Shepherd's Heart Music (Admin. by WORD MUSIC). All right reserved. Used by permission.

Appendix A
Abba! Father!

1. See Joachim Jeremias, *The Prayers of Jesus* (Philadelphia, PA: Fortress Press, 1978), 57–65.
2. Ibid., 57.
3. Ibid., 62.

Appendix B
Does God Love Himself?

1. J. I. Packer, *Hot Tub Religion* (Wheaton, IL: Tyndale House, 1987), 42.
2. Piper, *Desiring God*, 32.
3. Packer, *Hot Tub Religion*, 38.
4. Piper, *Desiring God*, 32.
5. Ibid., 34.
6. Ibid., 36.
7. Ibid.
8. Ibid.
9. C. S. Lewis, *Reflections on the Psalms* (San Diego, CA: Harcourt Brace Jovanovich, 1958), 95.
10. Piper, *Desiring God*, 37.
11. Ibid.

Two books by Mike Bickle

Passion for Jesus

As a young man, Mike Bickle was consumed with zeal for the gospel. Taught by his father to train hard and go for broke, it was no surprise that when Mike became a Christian, his commitment was total. He memorised whole chapters of the Bible; he prayed for hours; he fasted; he 'witnessed' fervently to others about his faith.

Passion for Jesus tells how the grace of God set Mike free and led him into the birthright of every believer – a knowledge of God's overpowering and intimate love.

> 'Anyone who knows Mike Bickle knows that he has subordinated everything in his life to this one goal: acquiring a passion for Jesus. And therein lies the power of this book.'
>
> – JACK DEERE

Growing in the Prophetic

Mike Bickle has known both the exhilaration and the confusion caused by prophetic ministry. As a young pastor not personally inclined towards prophecy, he was taken by surprise by the upsurge of the gift in his own church. Feeling almost ambushed by God, he looked for help and advice, but with little success. Thus began an often painful journey away from 'prophetic chaos' towards a clearer understanding of God's order. It is out of this experience he now writes for all those who are keen to see prophetic ministry developed in the church today.

Kingsway Publications

Two books by Dr Jack Deere

Surprised by the Power of the Spirit

What caused a professor in a conservative evangelical theological college to change his mind about the Holy Spirit so radically that he had to leave?

Much more than an explanation of why one theologian came to believe in signs and wonders for today, this is a profound biblical apologetic, arguing carefully and courteously for the view that the Holy Spirit's supernatural gifts did not cease in New Testament times. And Dr Deere serves Christians on both sides of the debate, as he marks out pitfalls which threaten to hinder the present-day supernatural ministry of the Holy Spirit.

'Solidly anchored in the Bible.' – WAYNE GRUDEM

'This is a book whose time has come.' – JOHN WHITE

Surprised by the Voice of God

This book is written for ordinary Christians who want to hear God's voice above the clamour of everyday life. But how do we tell when it is God speaking to us, and not our emotions, or the opinions of others, or even dark spiritual forces?

Jack Deere brings together inspiring stories from people who have learned to trust God's voice today, his own experiences in teaching and pastoral ministry, and mature biblical teaching – all of which can help us to understand the Bible and to hear from God both for ourselves and for those to whom we minister.

'A refreshing and powerful word on the ministry of the prophetic. No one desiring to hear God's voice speaking today can afford to ignore this book.'
— LYNDON BOWRING

 Kingsway Publications